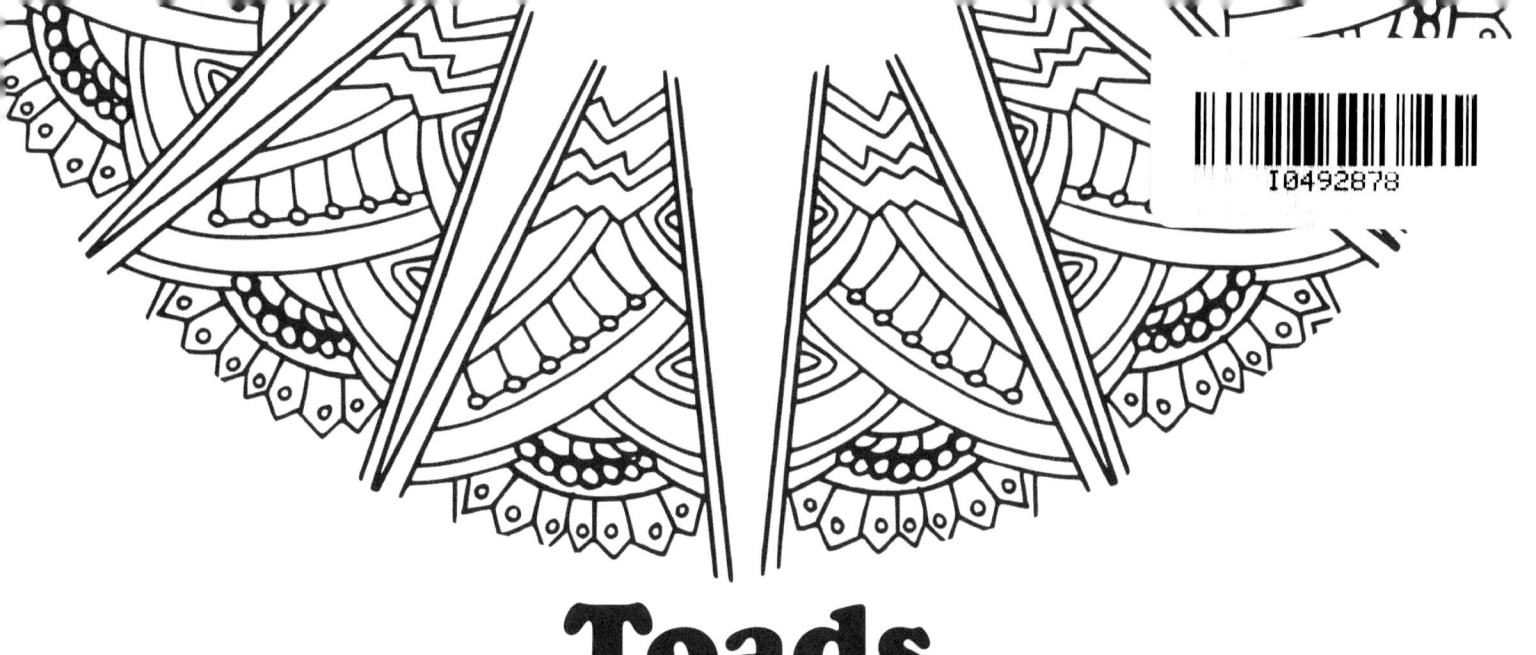

Toads Of History

Adult Coloring Book

J.D. Luke

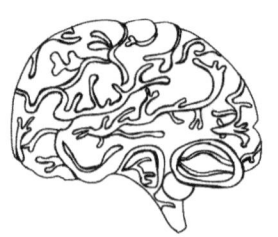

ISBN-13: 978-1533456700
ISBN-10: 1533456704

Color Test Page

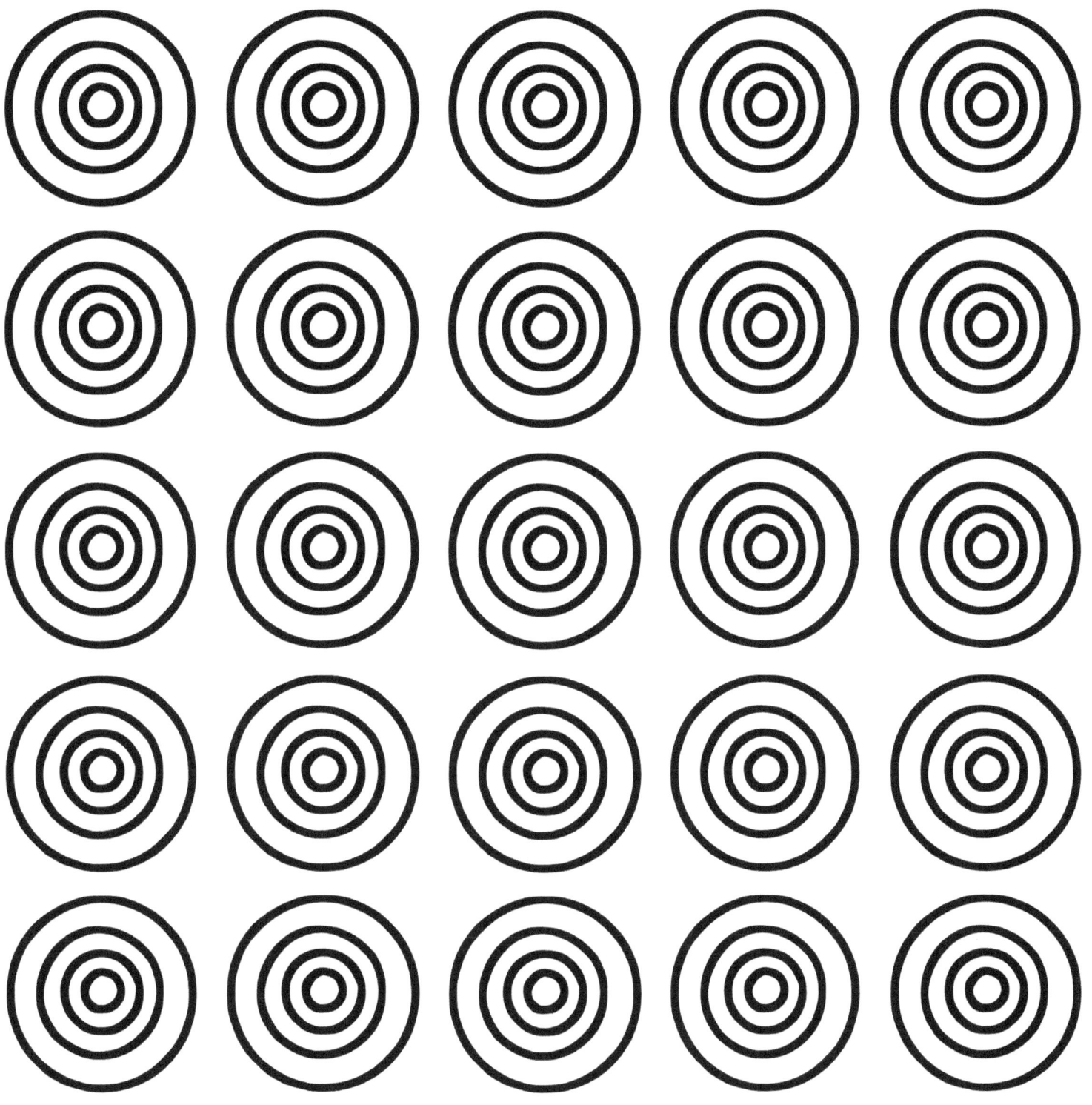

Color Test Page

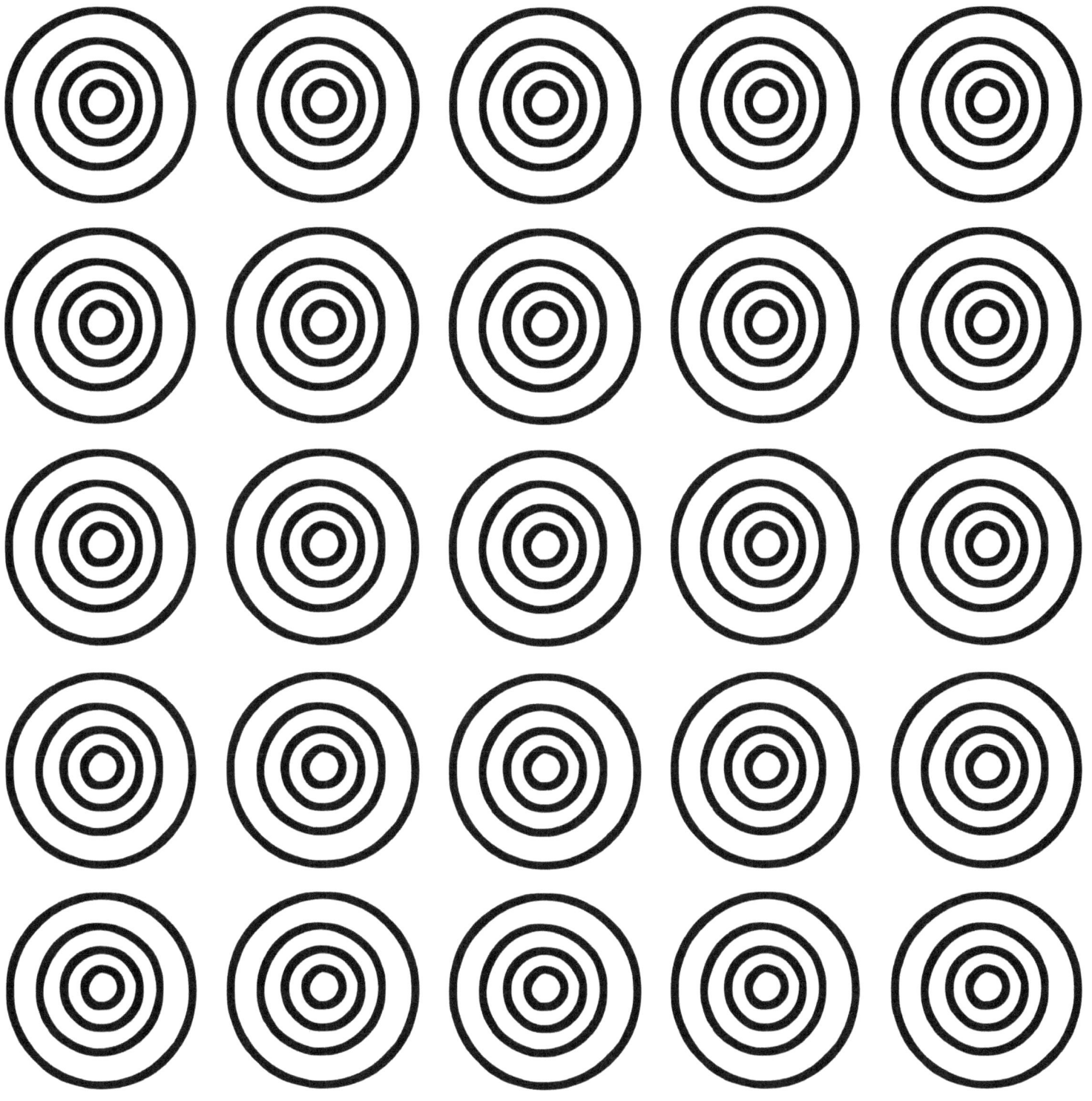

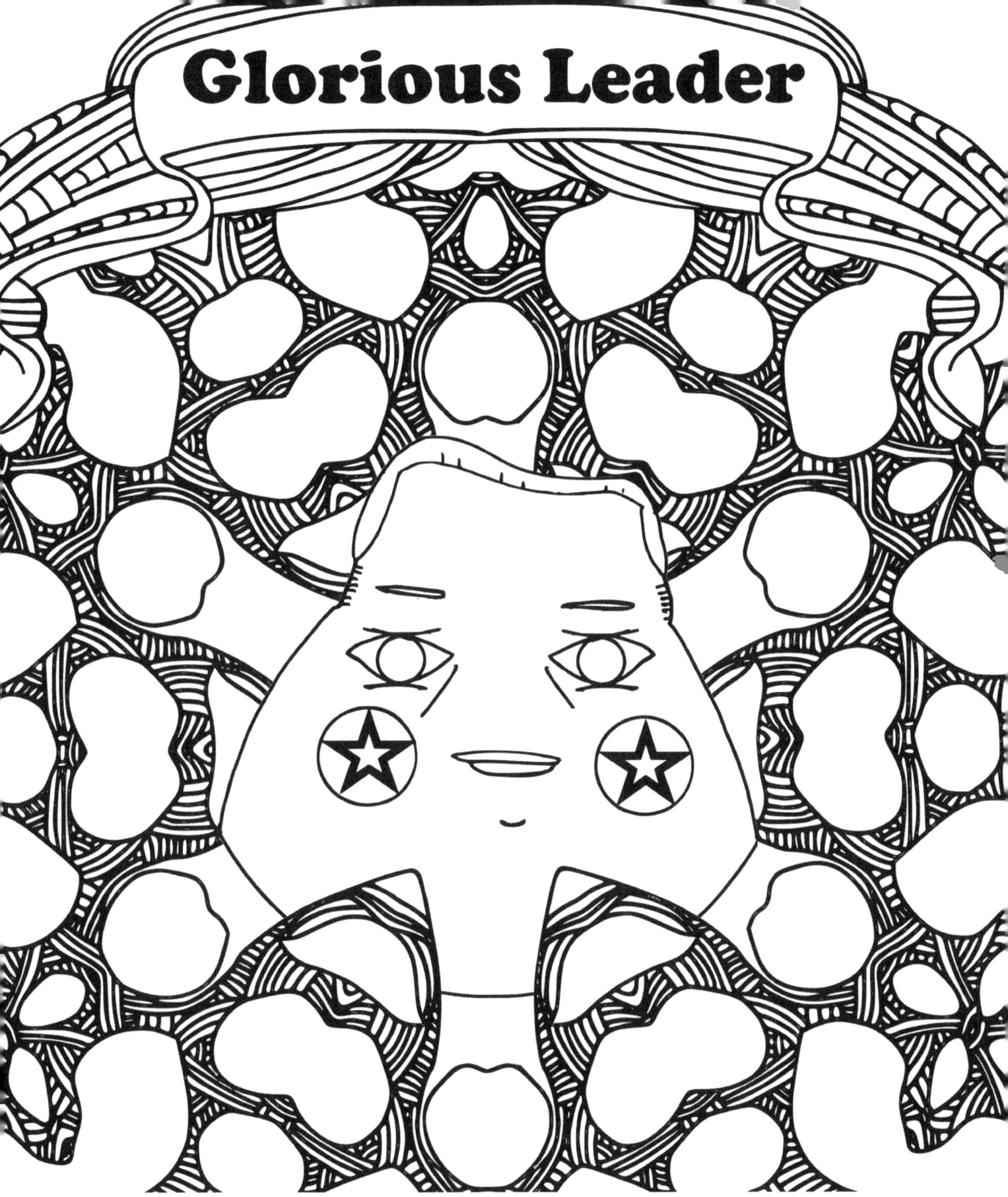

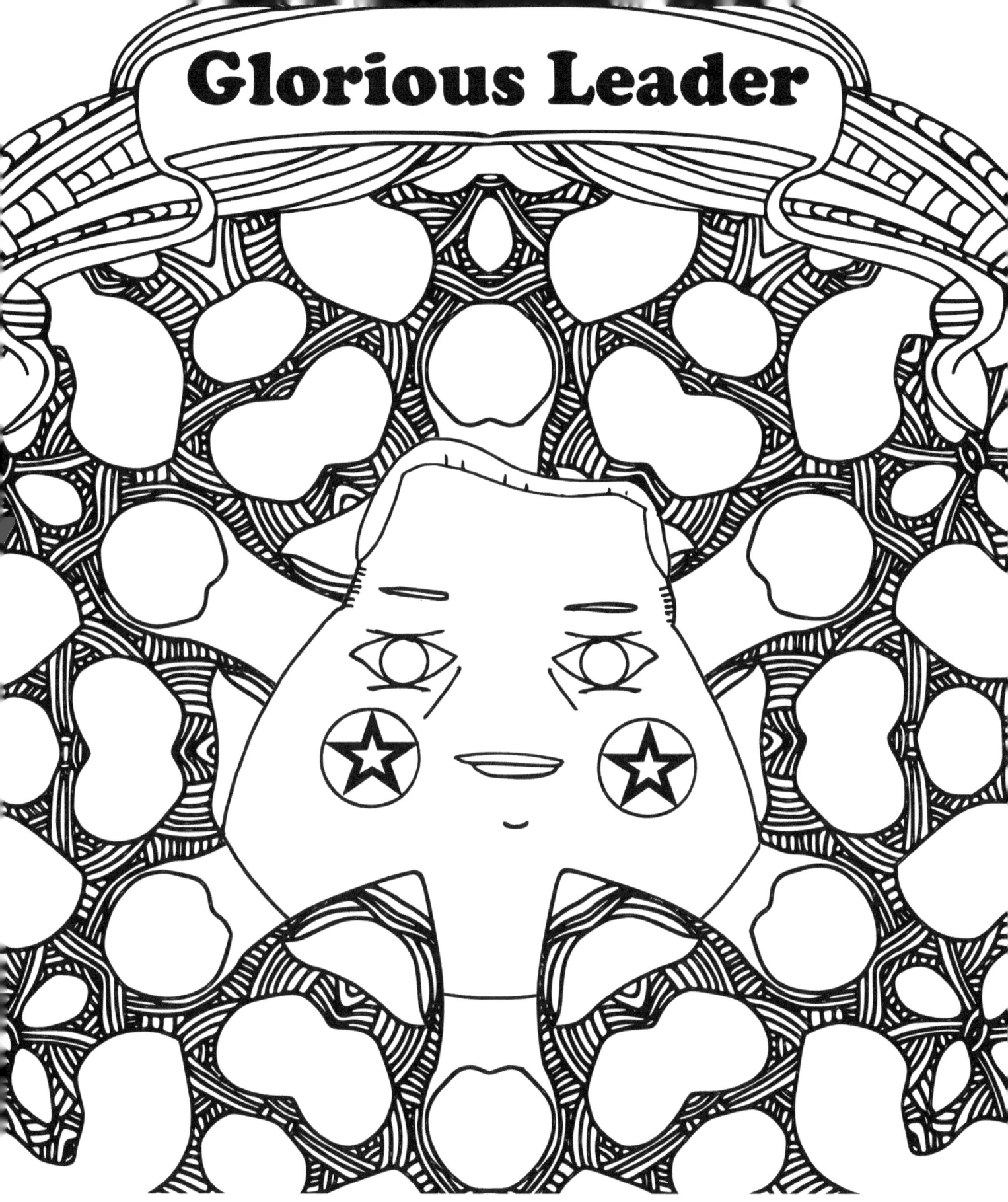

Slick Rick

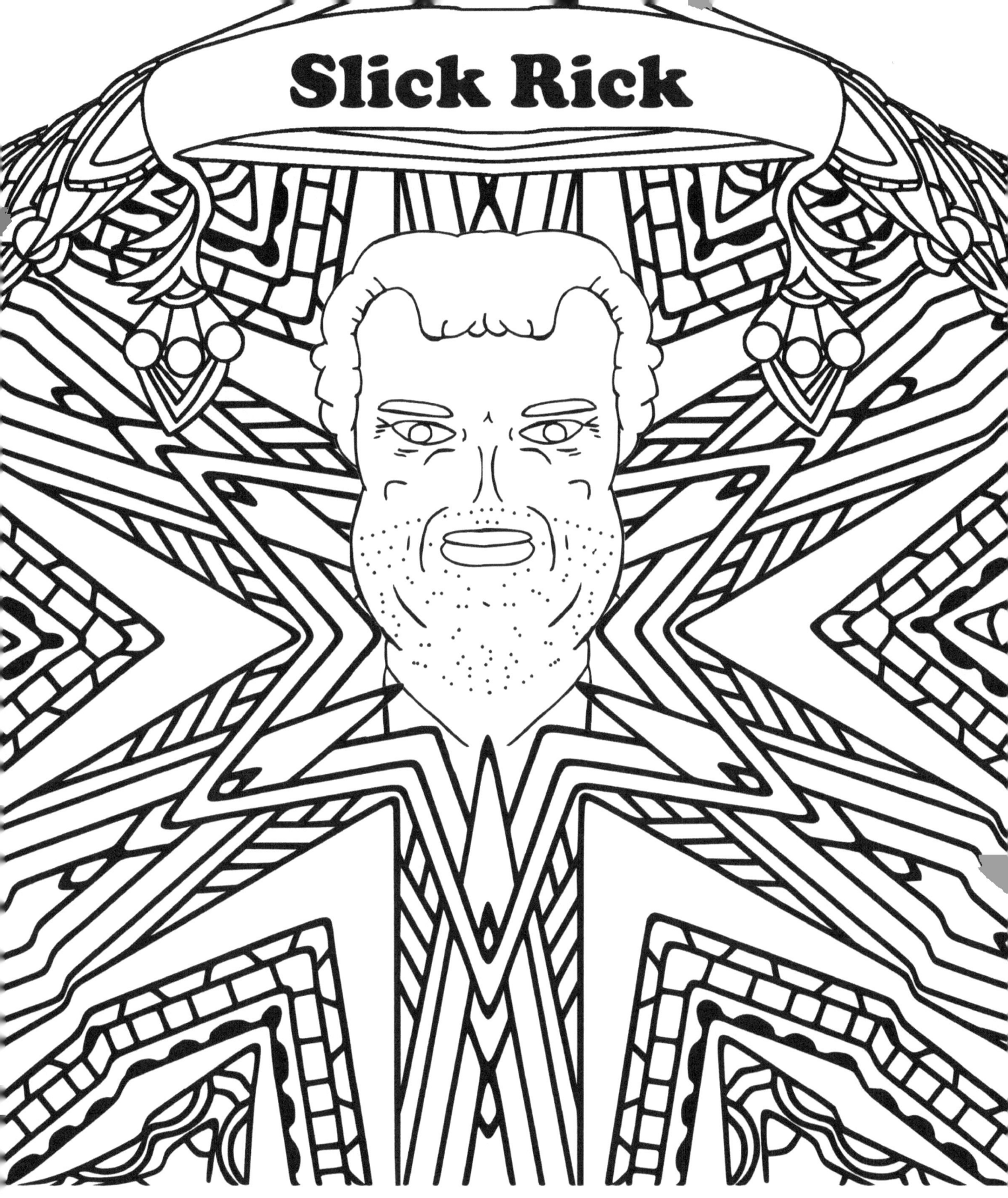

"I can take it. The tougher it gets, the cooler I get."

Tricky Dick

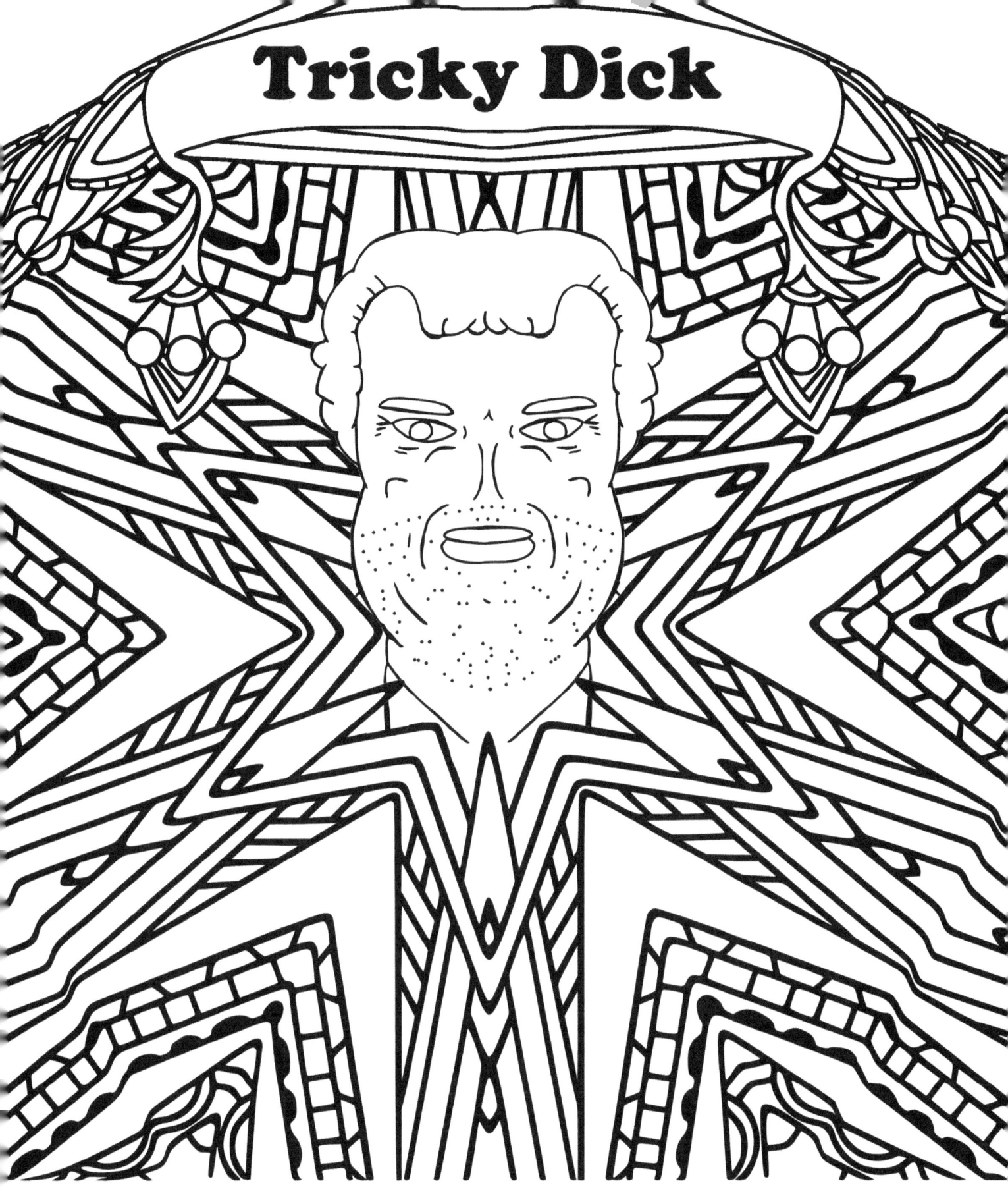

"Well, I screwed it up real good, didn't I?"

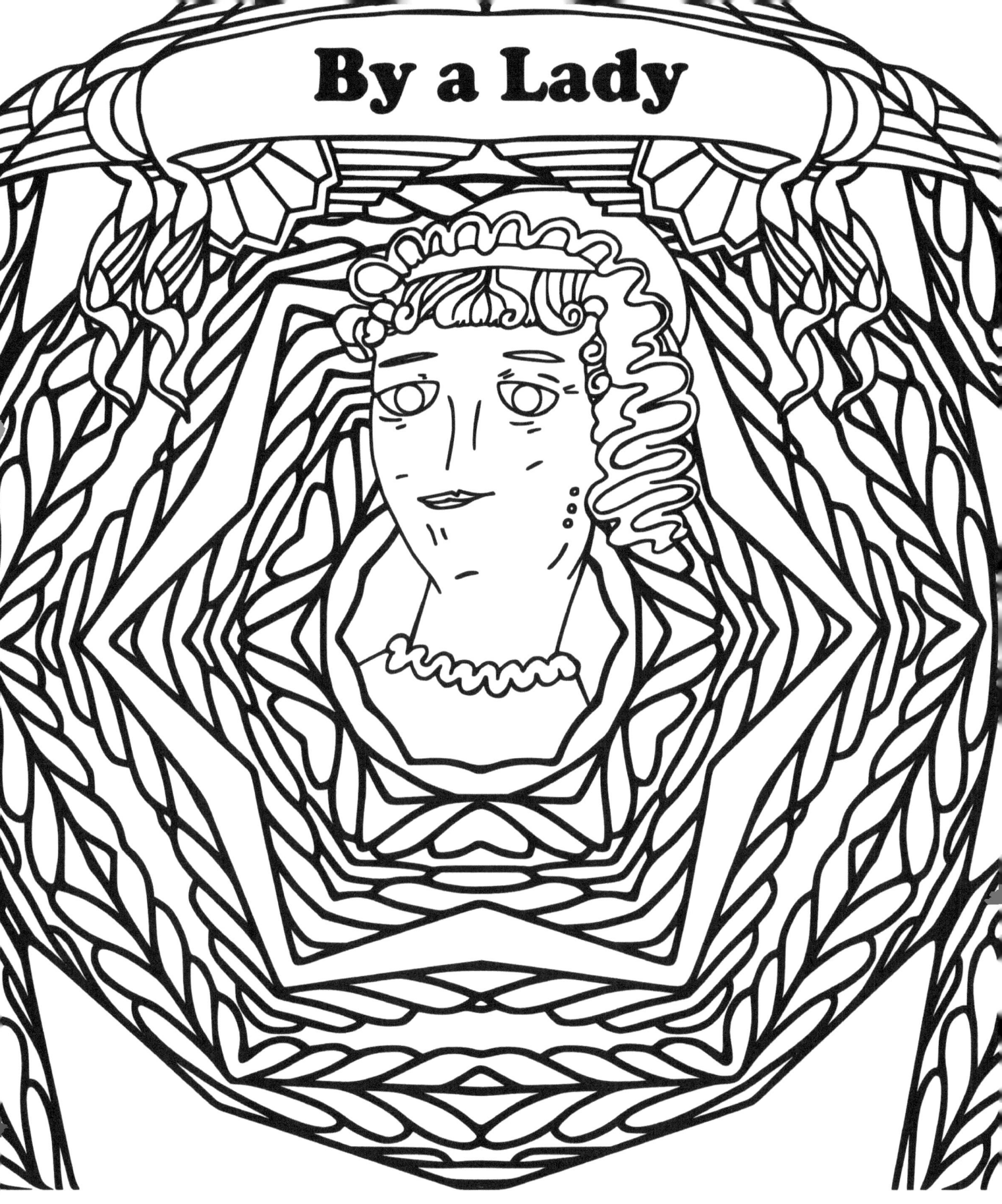

Jenny

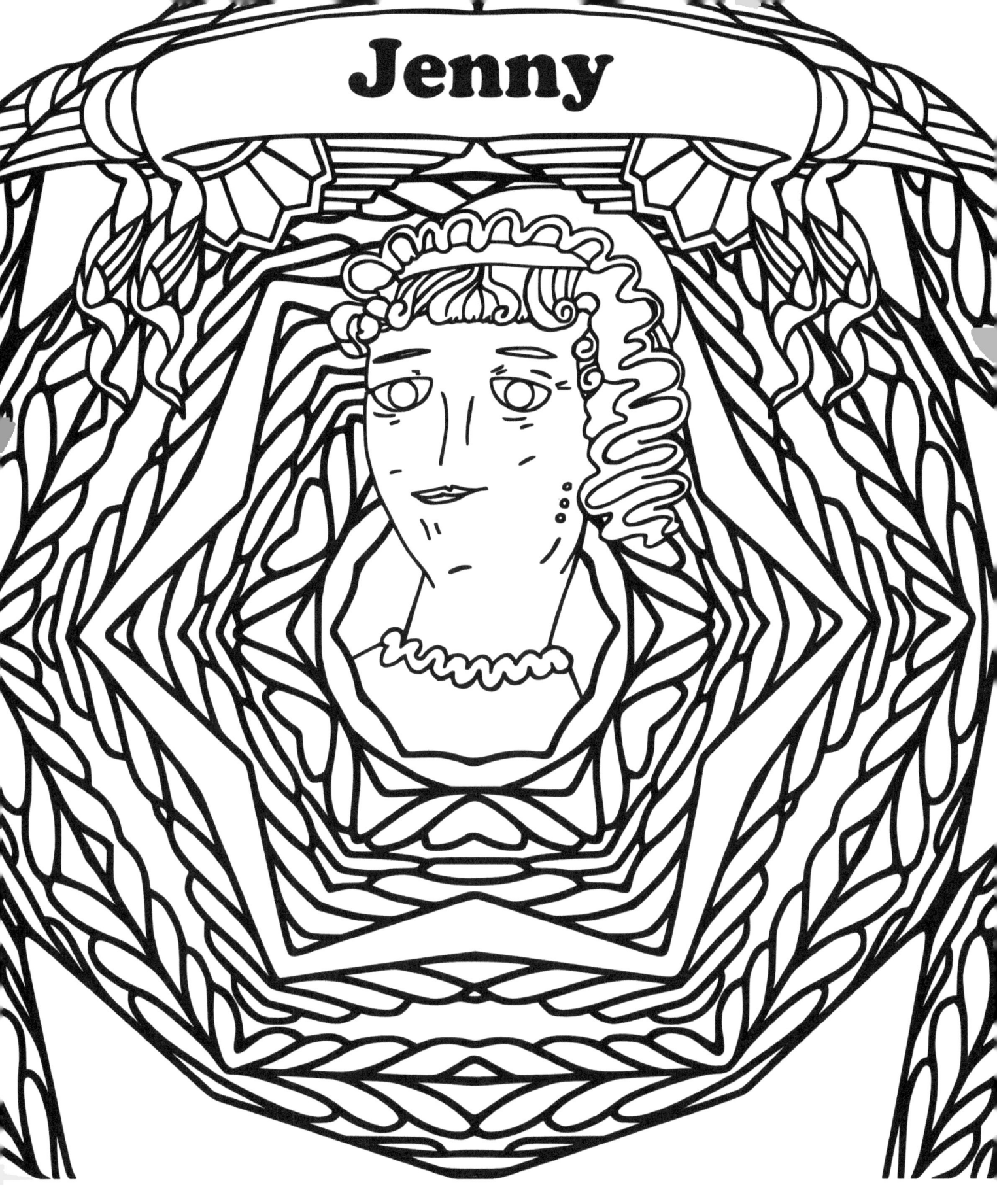

"Suck it Mark Twain!"

The Chairman

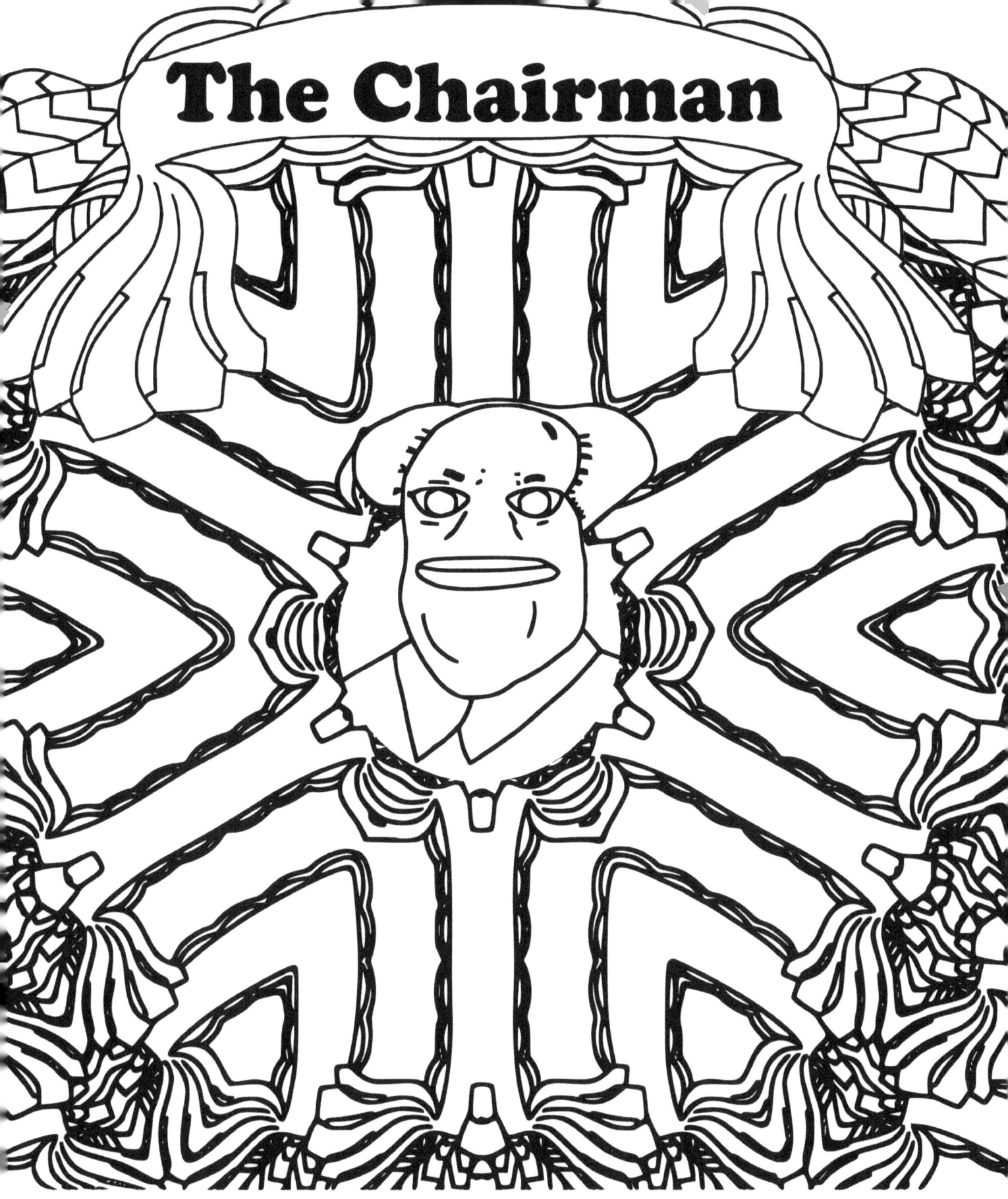

"Learn from the masses, and then teach them."

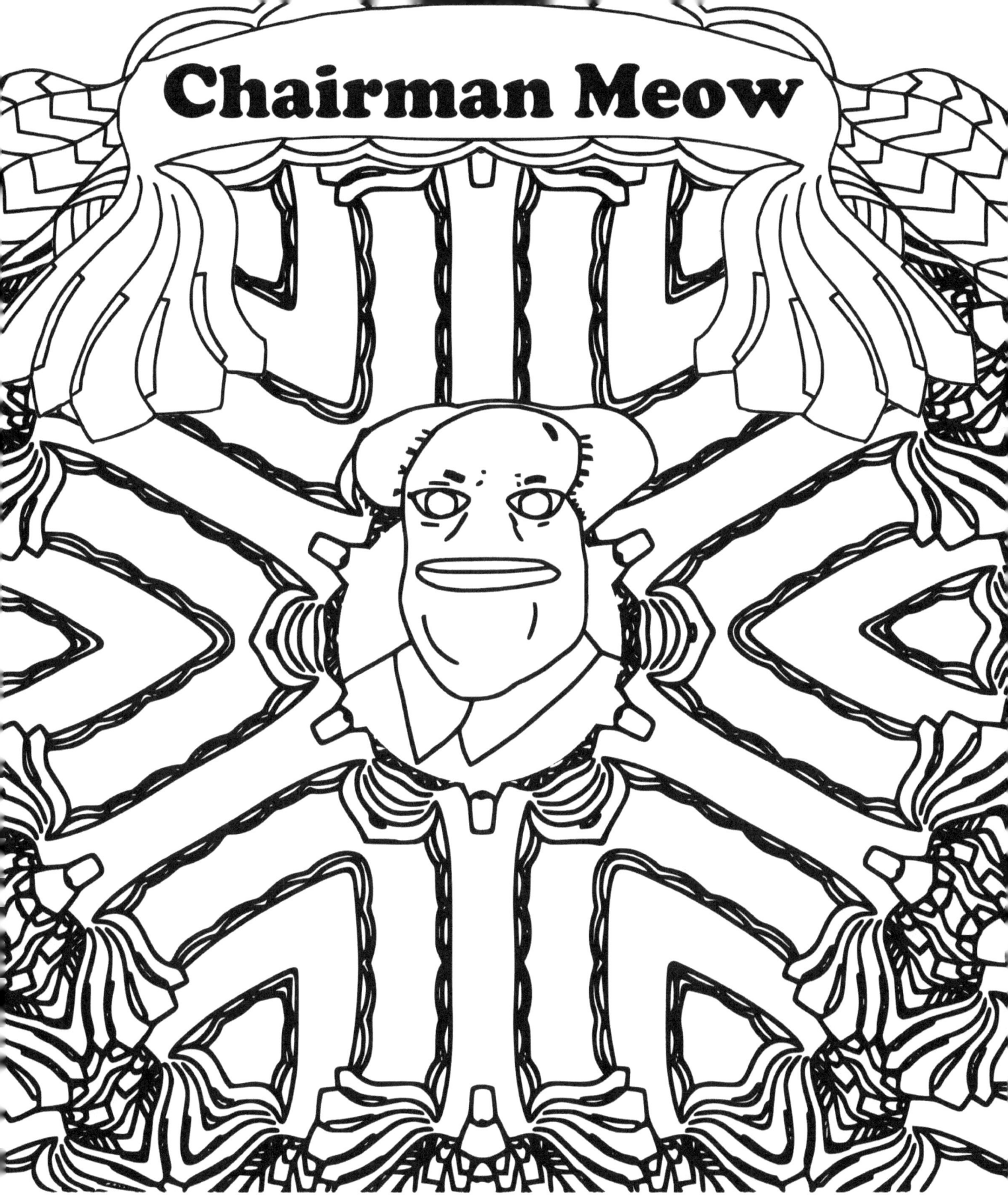

Chairman Meow

"To read too many books is harmful."

The Biggly Emperor

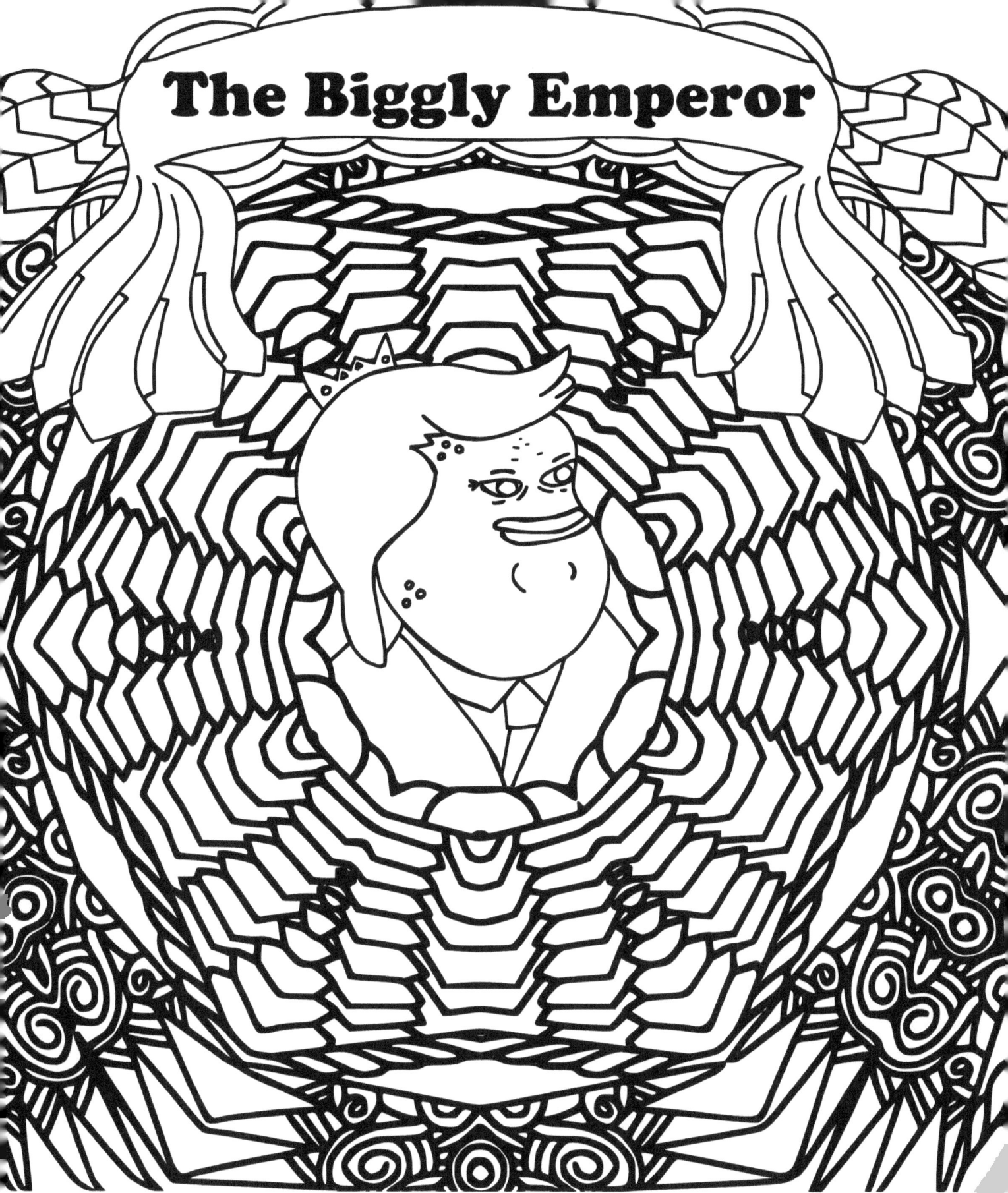

"I love the poorly educated."

The Nicknamer

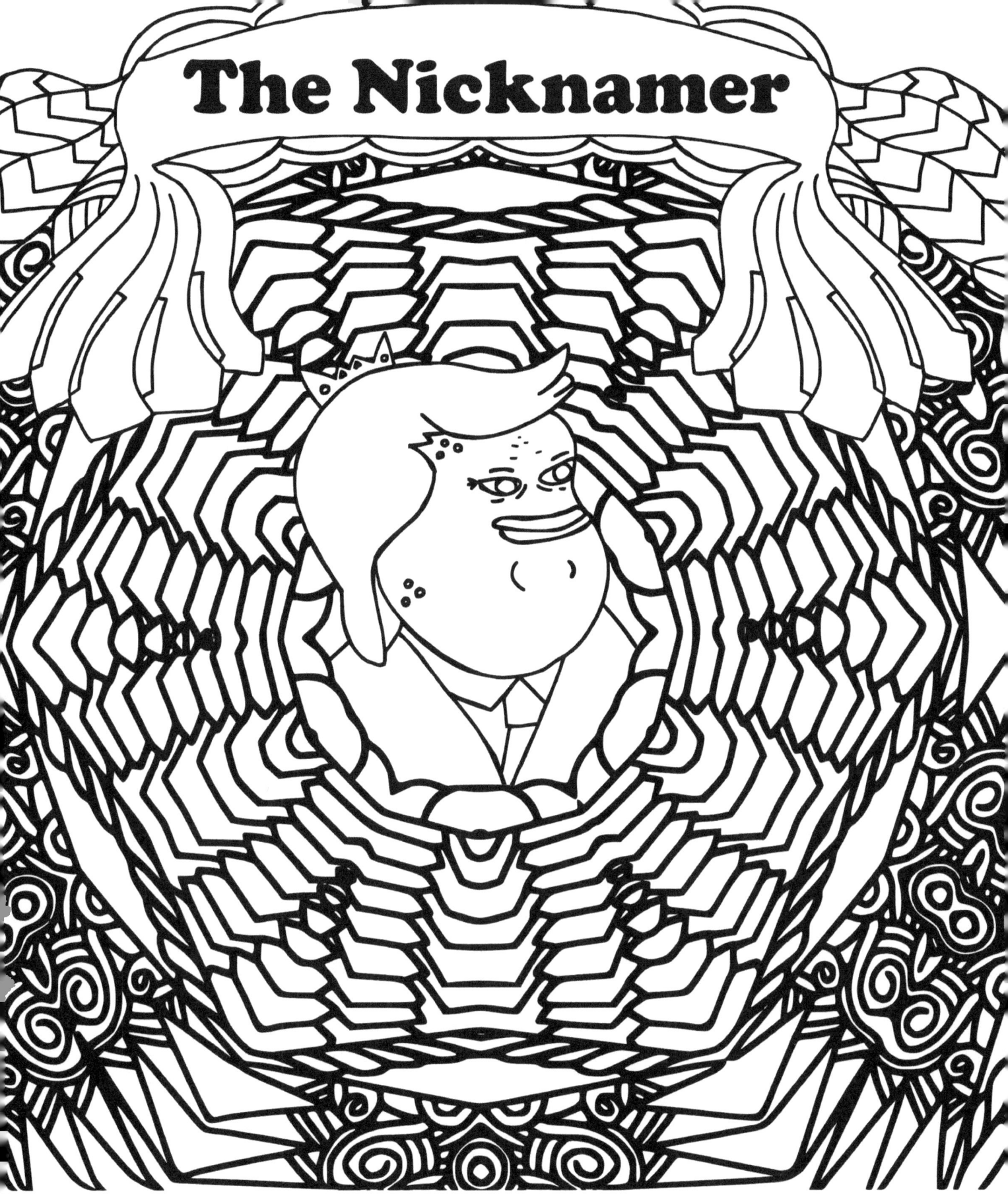

"That's one of the nice things. I mean, part of the beauty of me is that I'm very rich."

Rodham

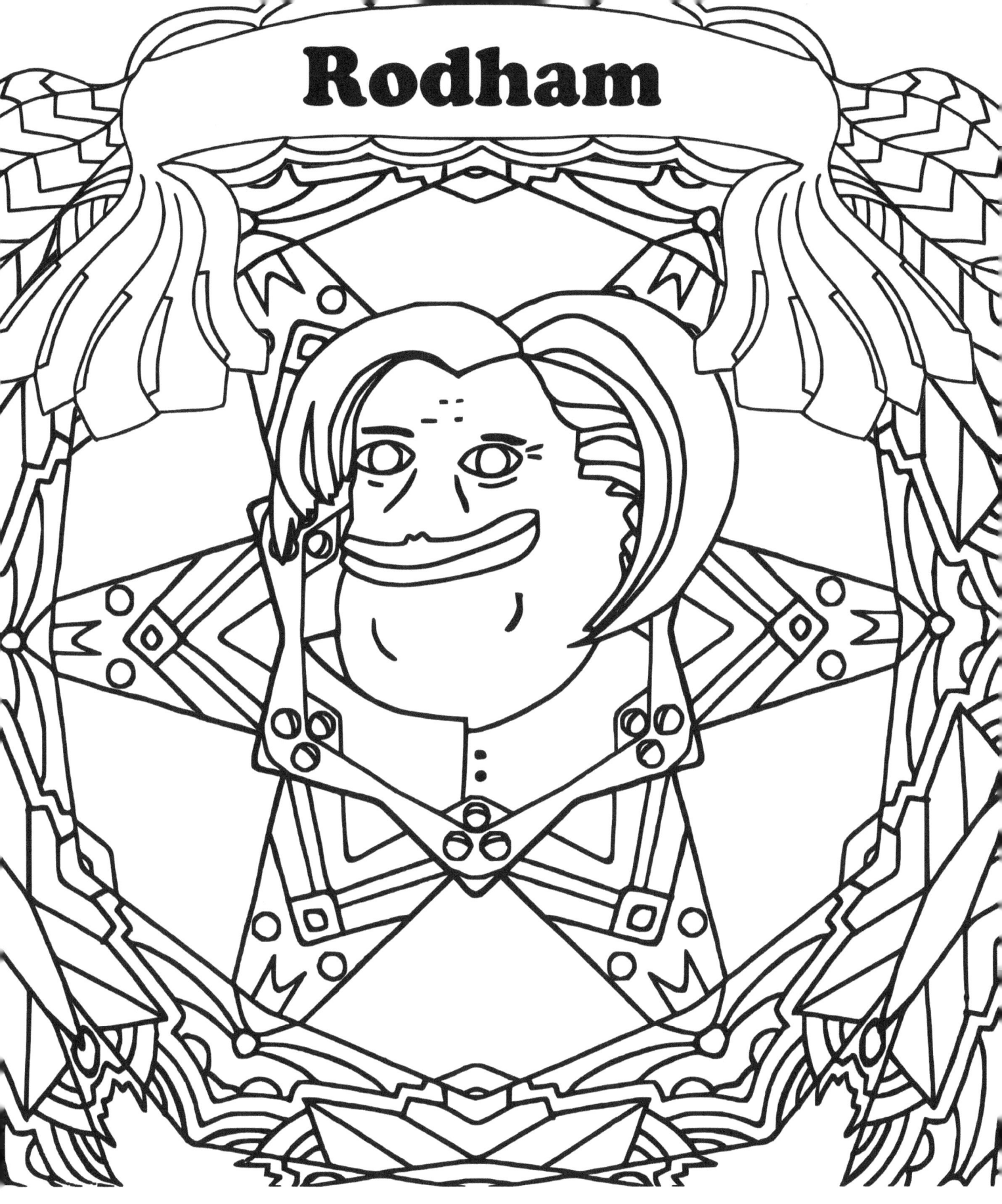

"We came, we saw, he died."

Madam Secretary

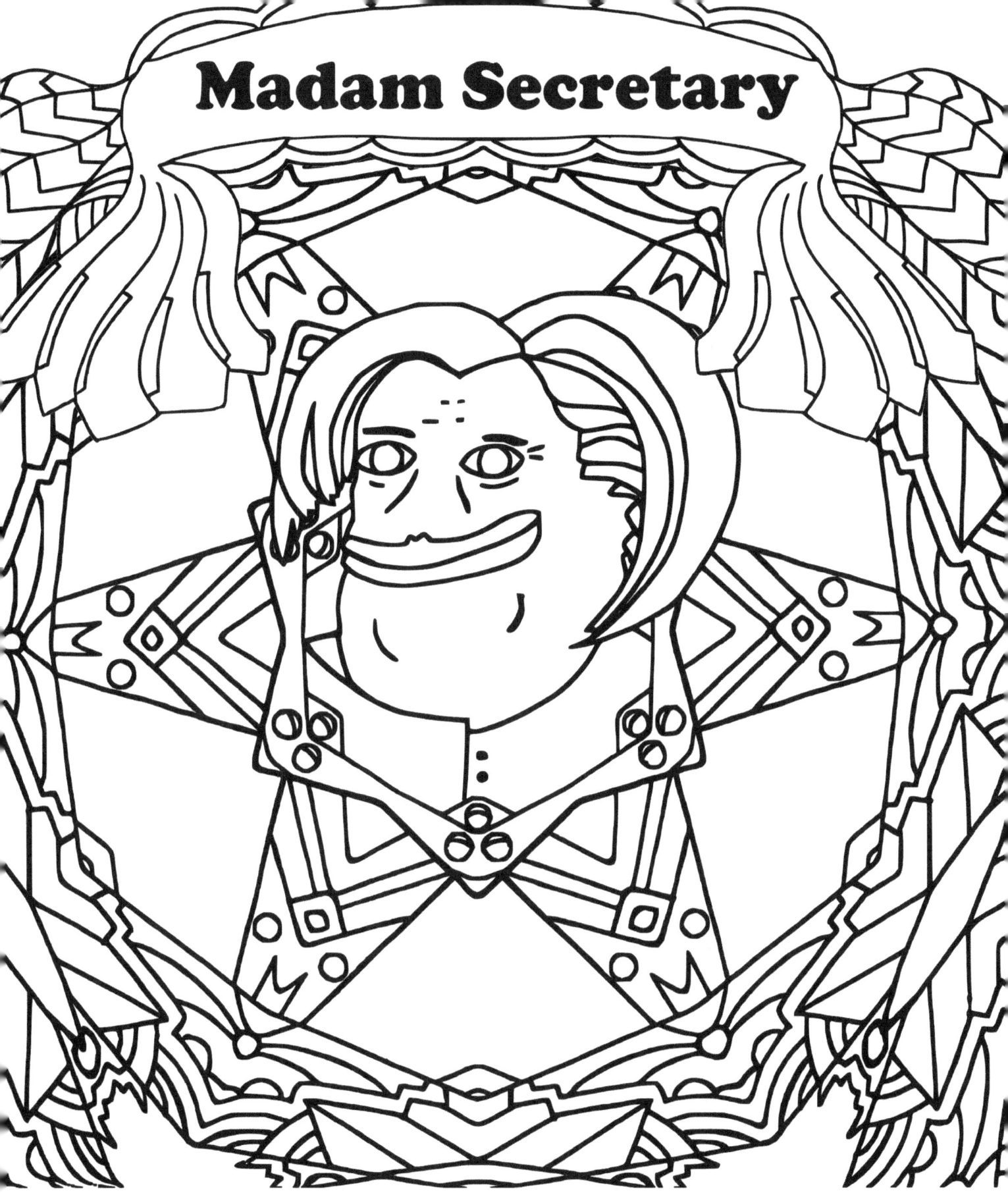

"Everyday Americans need a champion. I want to be that champion."

The Greater Good

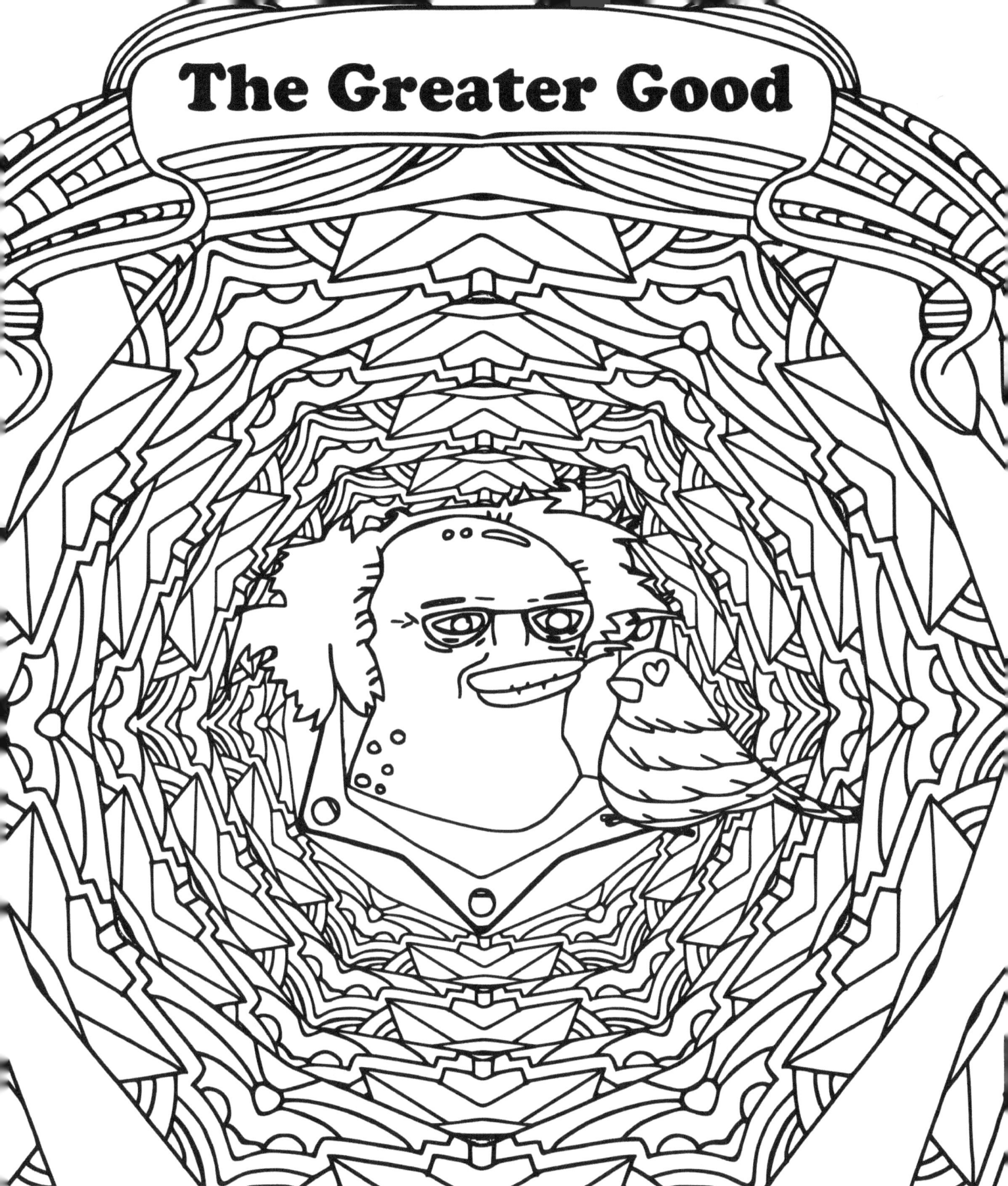

"Pay your damn dime!"

Social Democrat

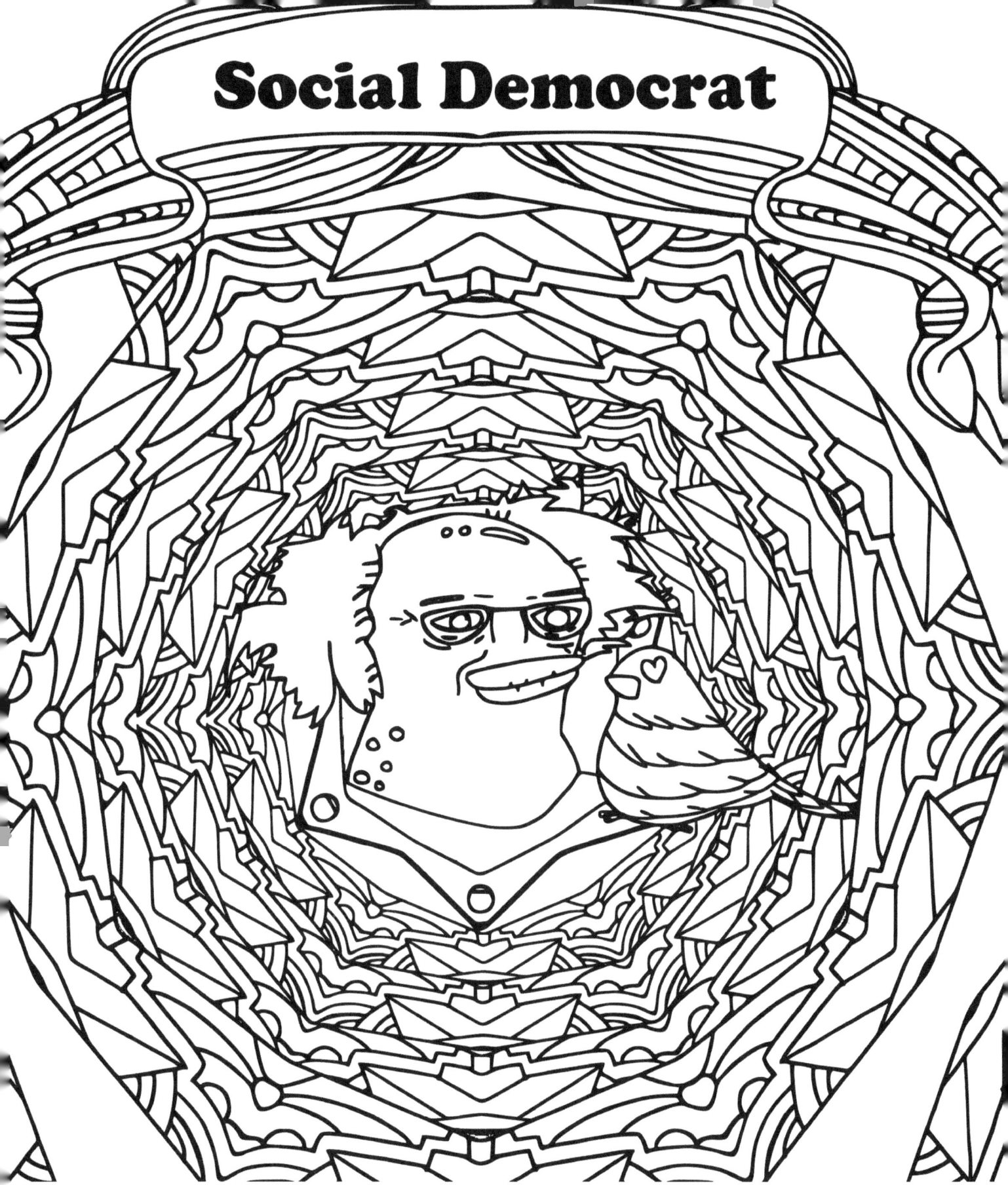

"We'll get it right this time."

Reason. Evidence. Hemlock.

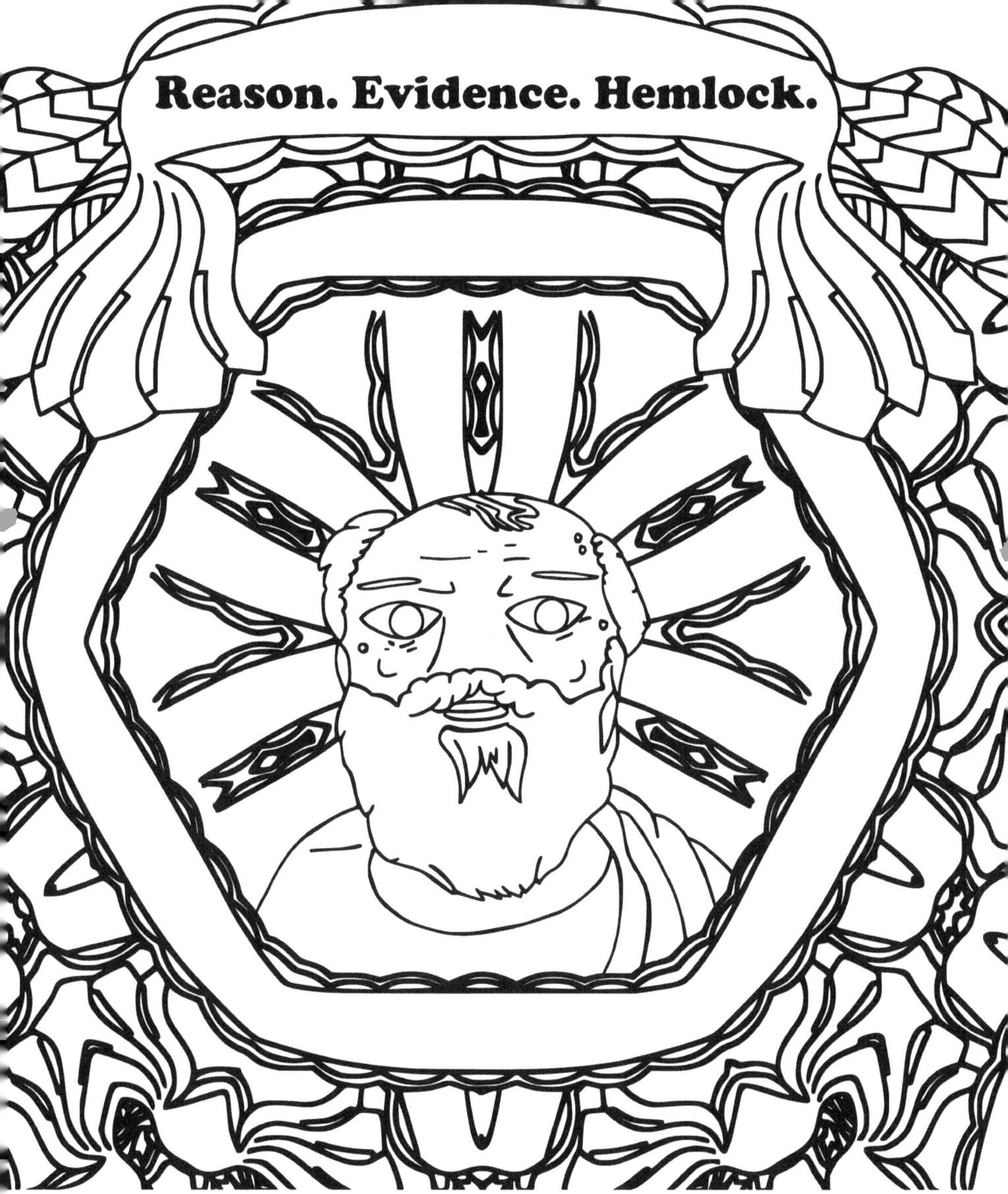

"Beware the barrenness of a busy life."

Gadfly

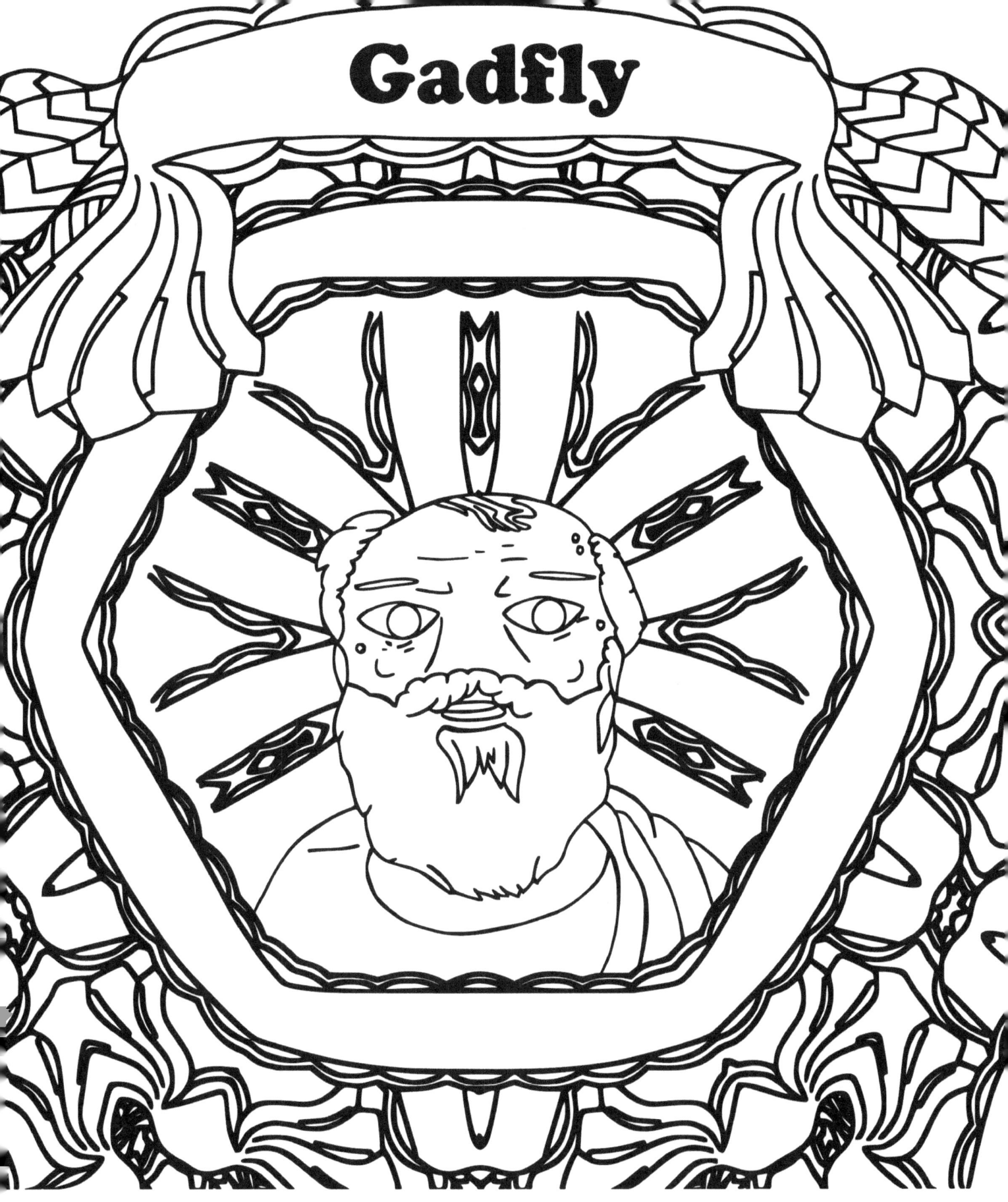

"Be as you wish to seem."

Dutch

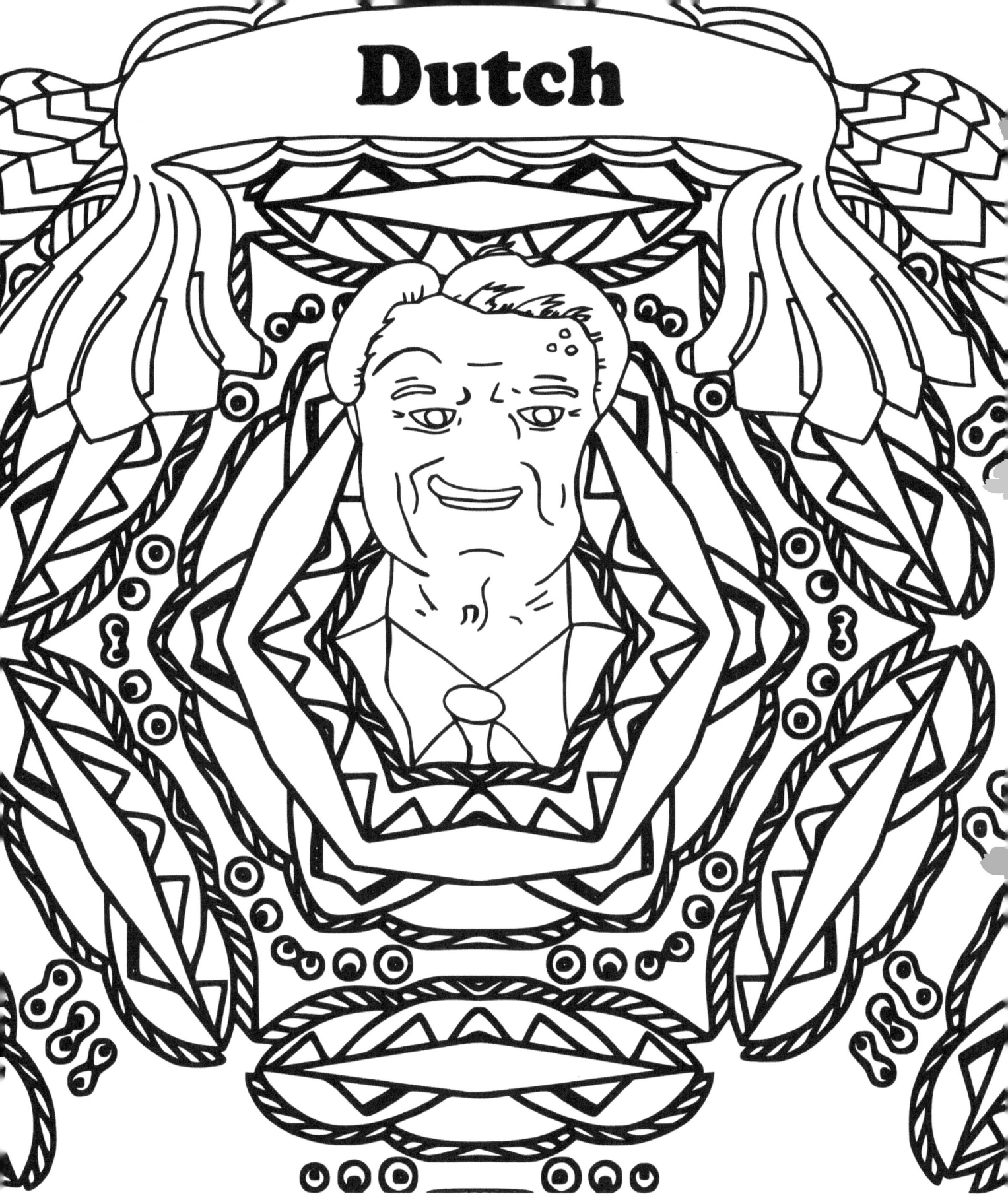

"Life is one grand, sweet song, so start the music."

Ronnie

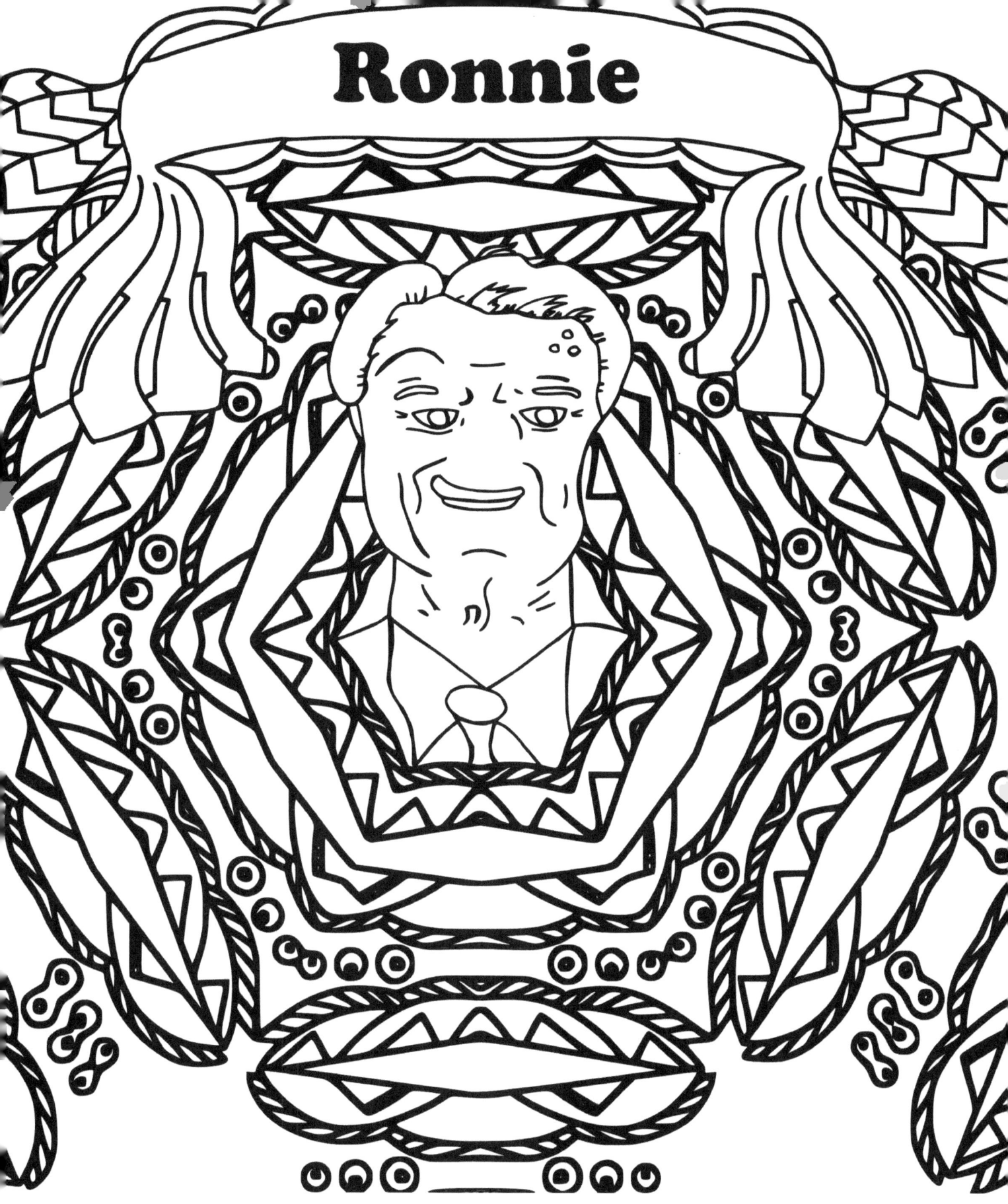

"I have left orders to be awakened."

Das Kapital

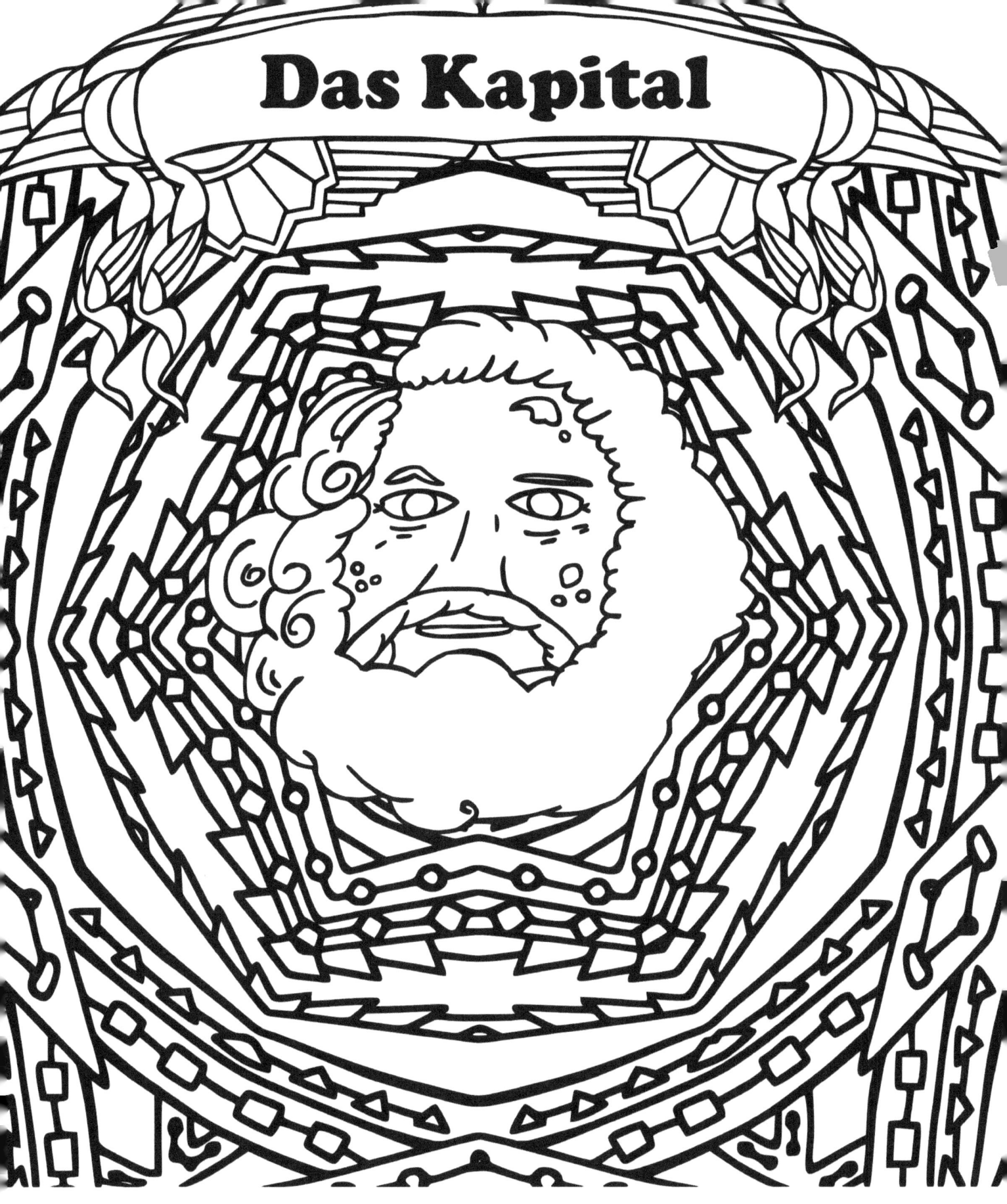

"Revolutions are the locomotives of history."

Karl Von Moor

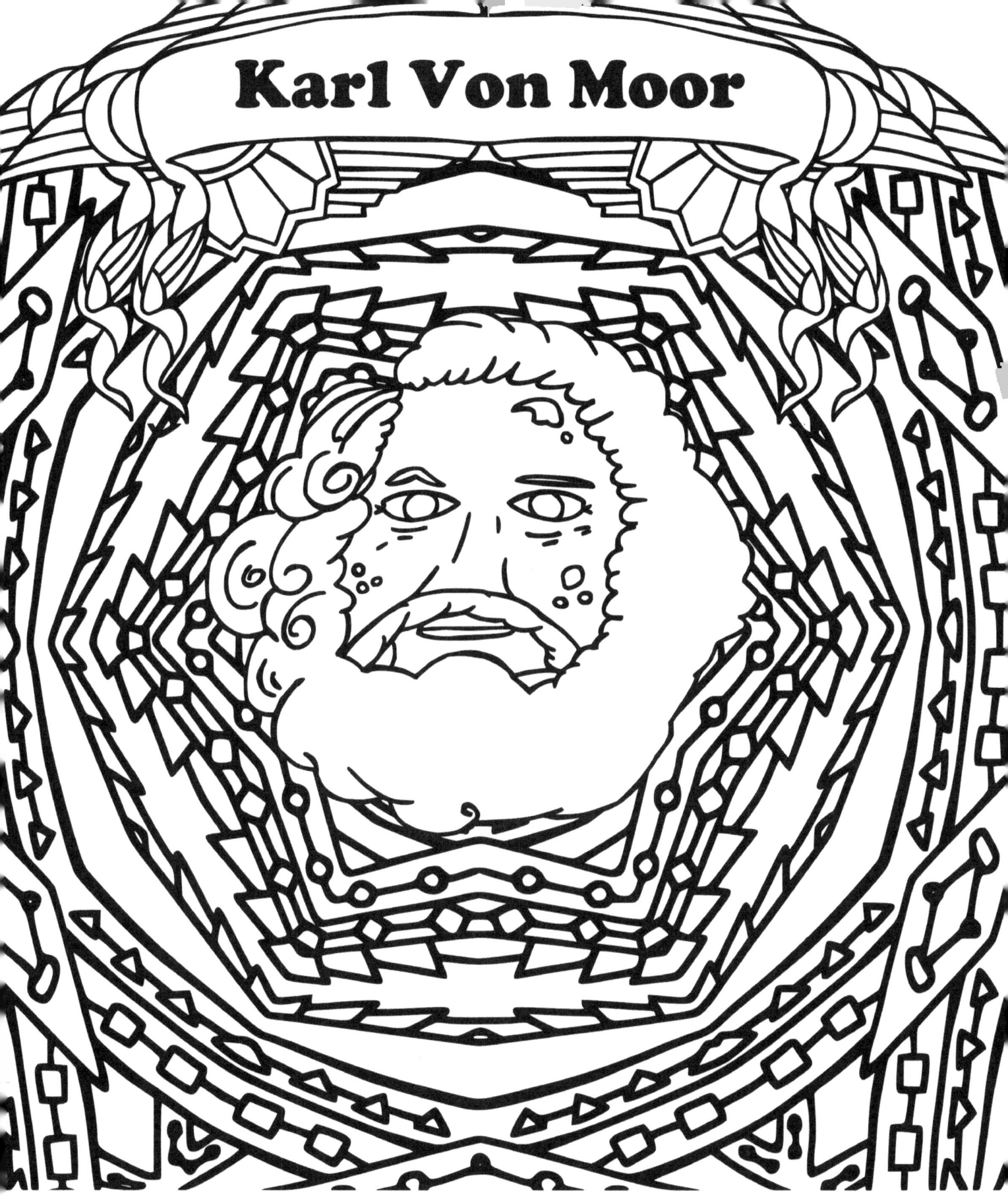

"Last words are for fools who haven't said enough."

The King

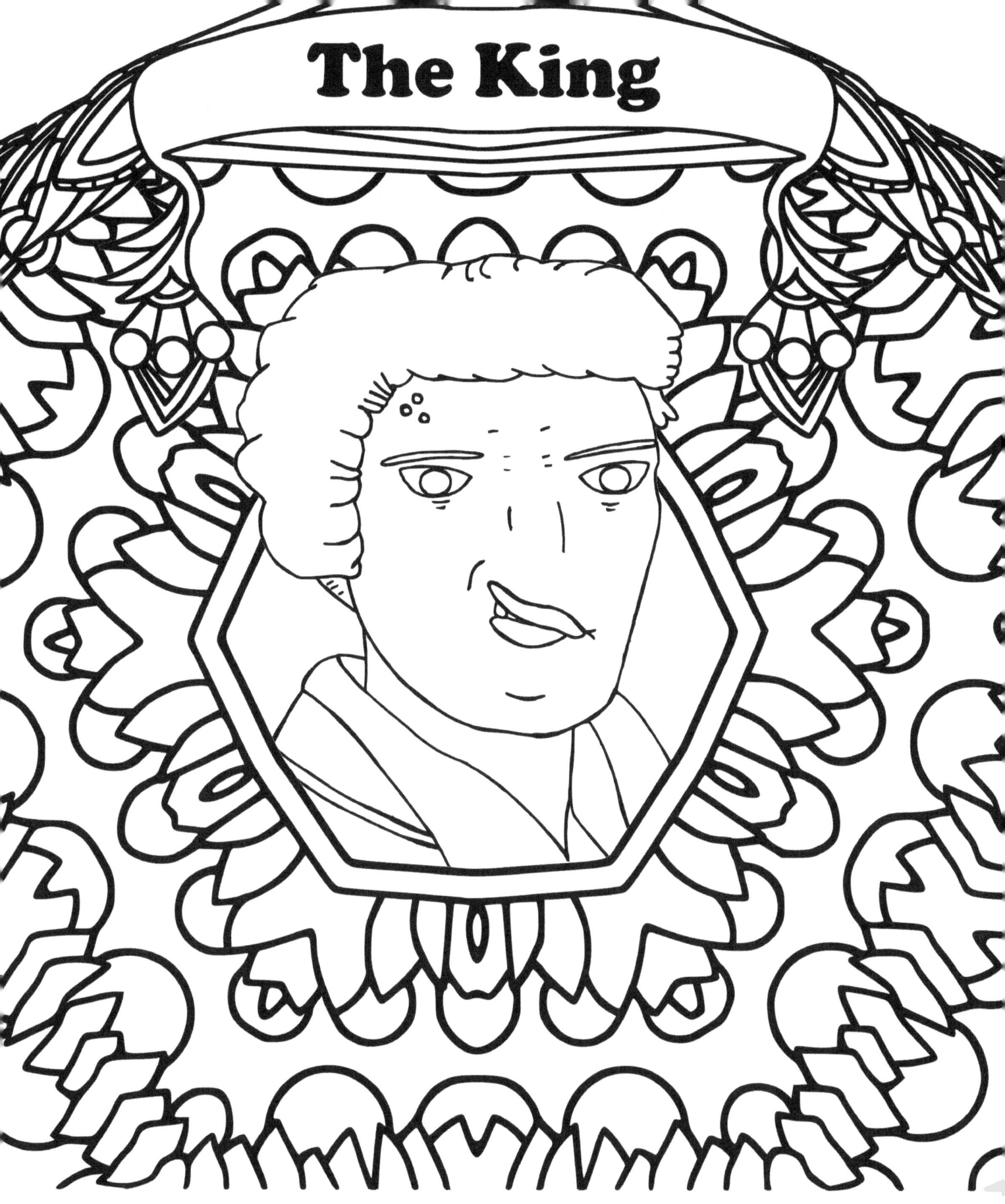

"Accountants over bodyguards."

Dr. Carpenter

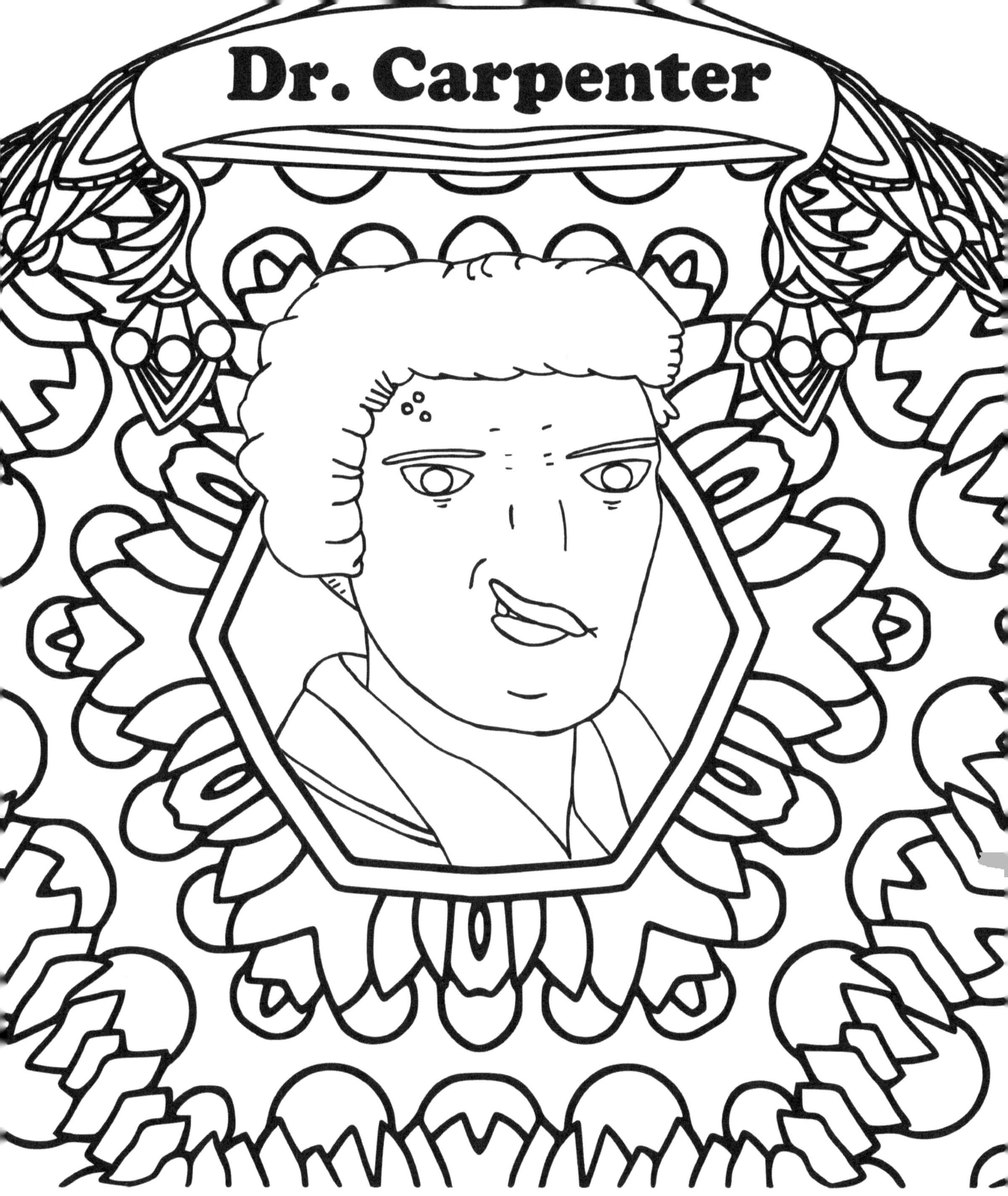

"Truth is like the sun. You can shut it out for a time, but it ain't goin' away."

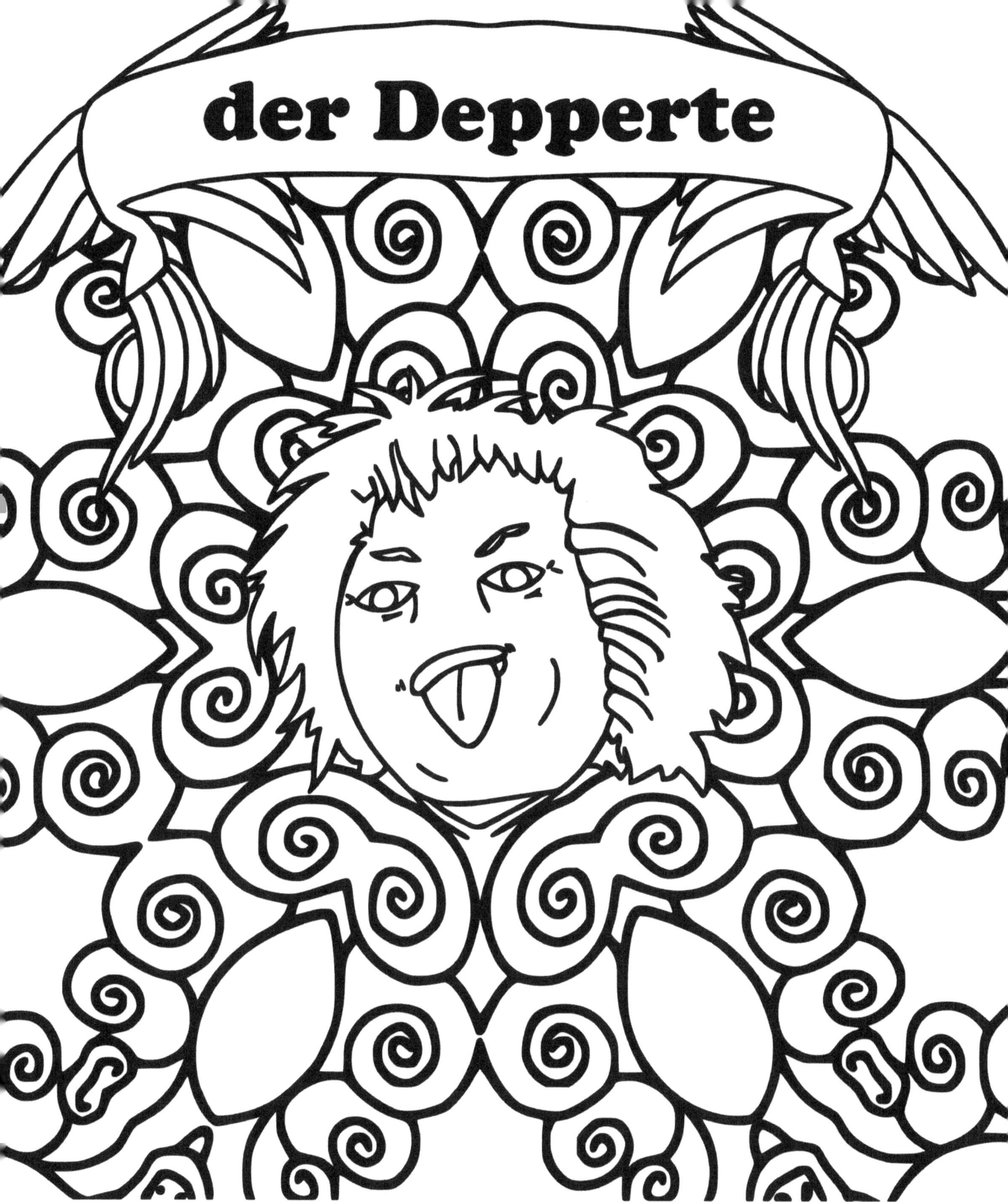

der Depperte

"Math isn't hard!"

der Depperte

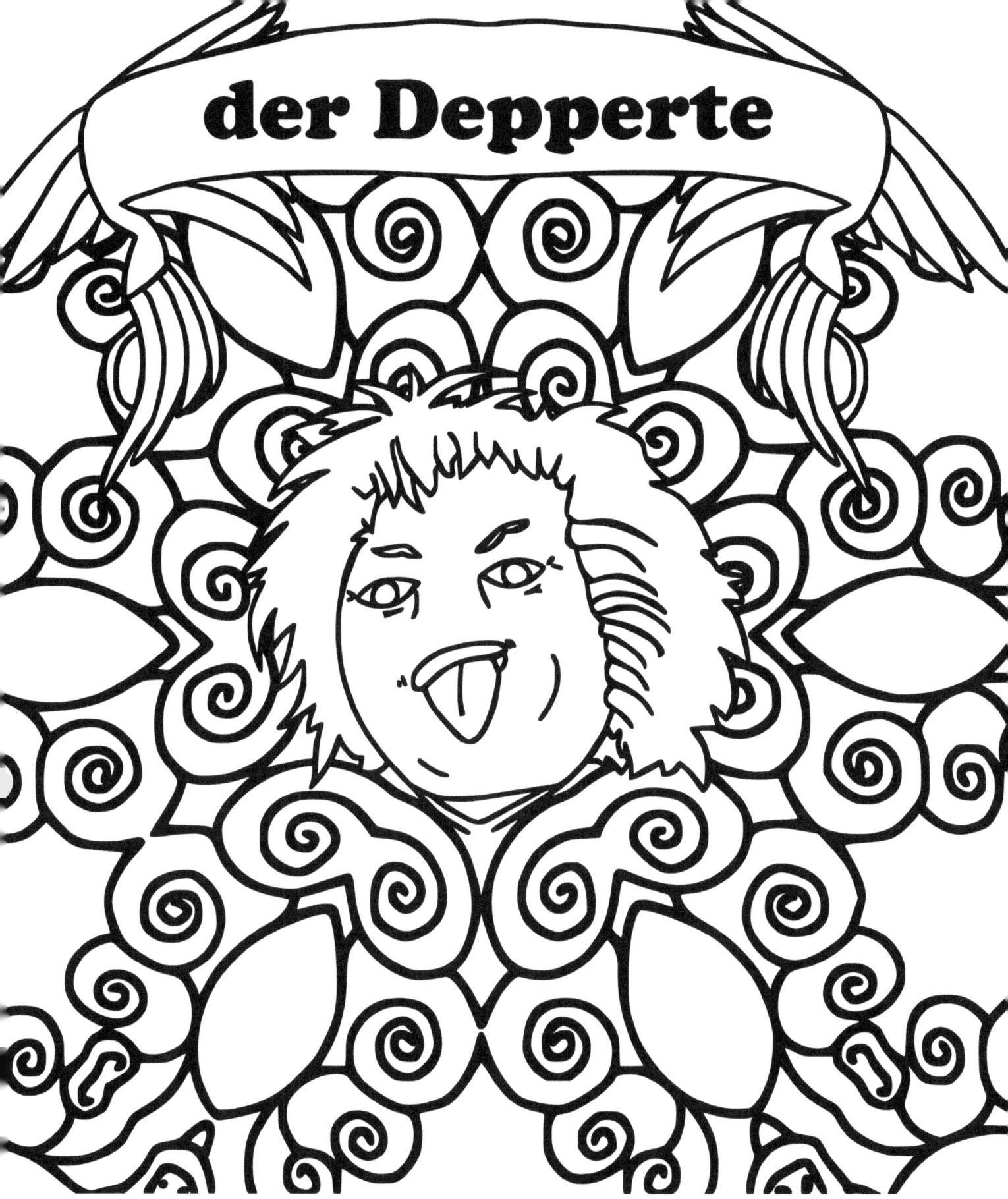

"Two things are infinite: the universe and human stupidity; and I'm not sure about the universe."

British Bulldog

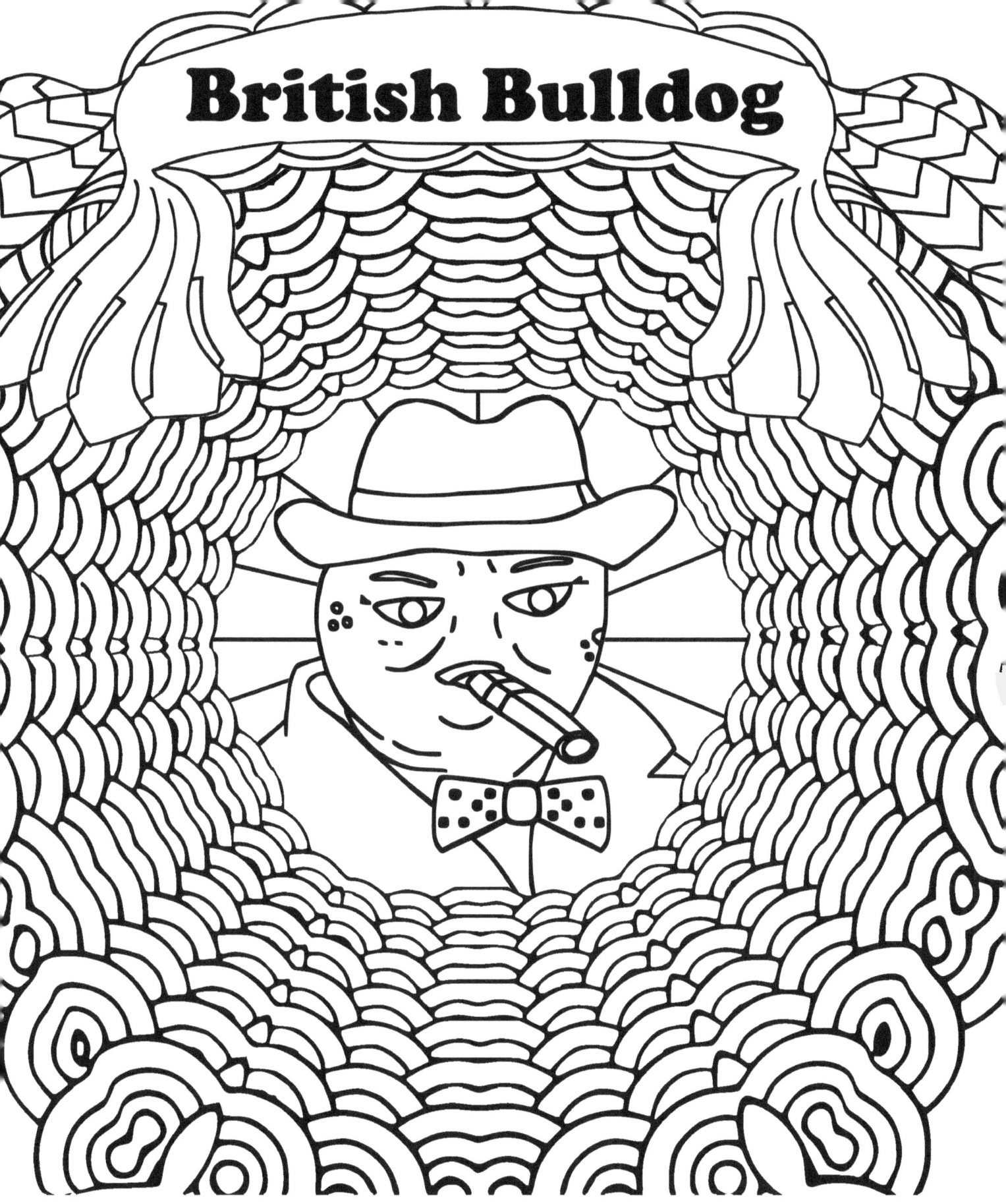

"If you're going through hell, keep going."

Winnie

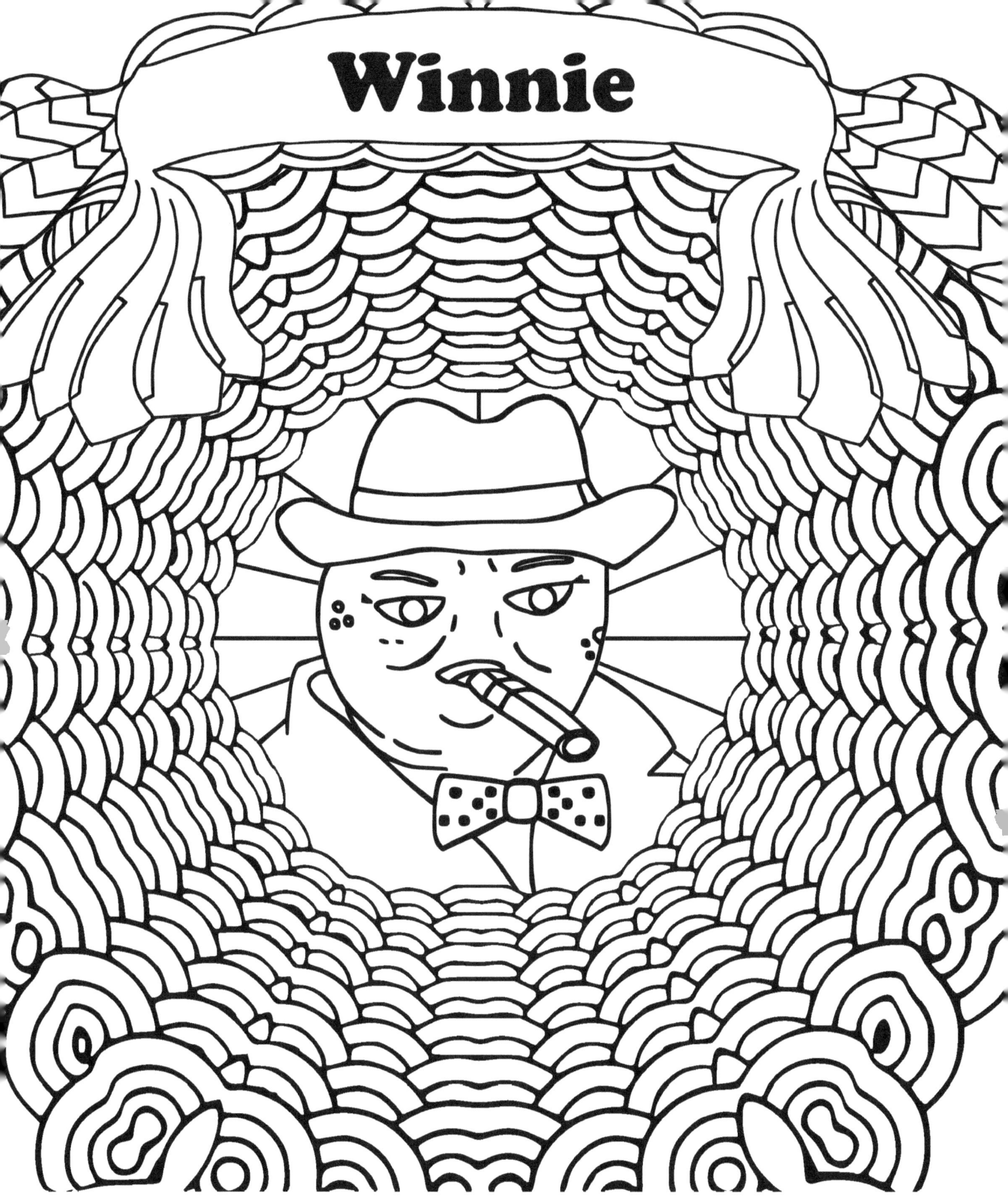

"Attitude is a little thing that makes a big difference."

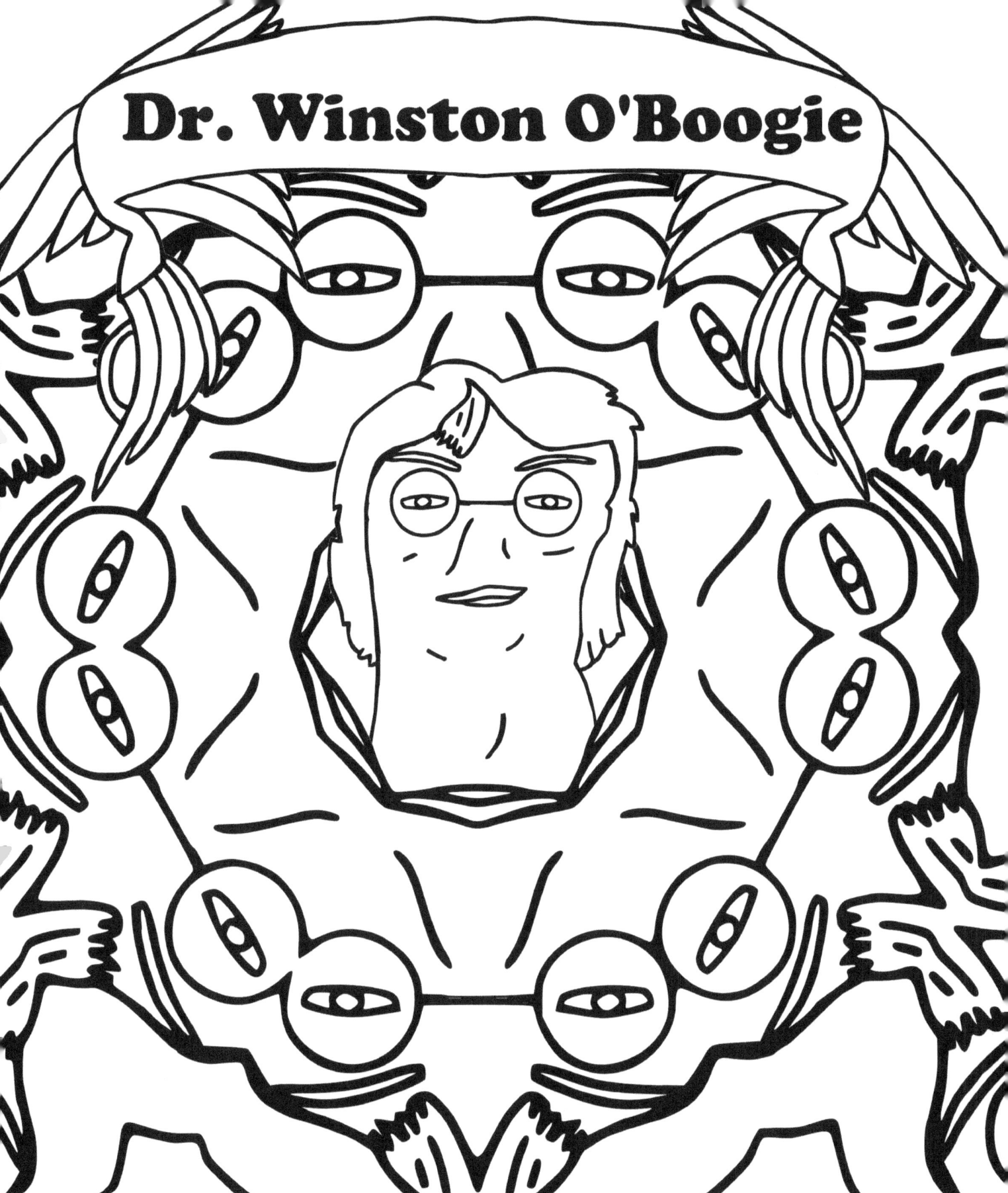

Lennon

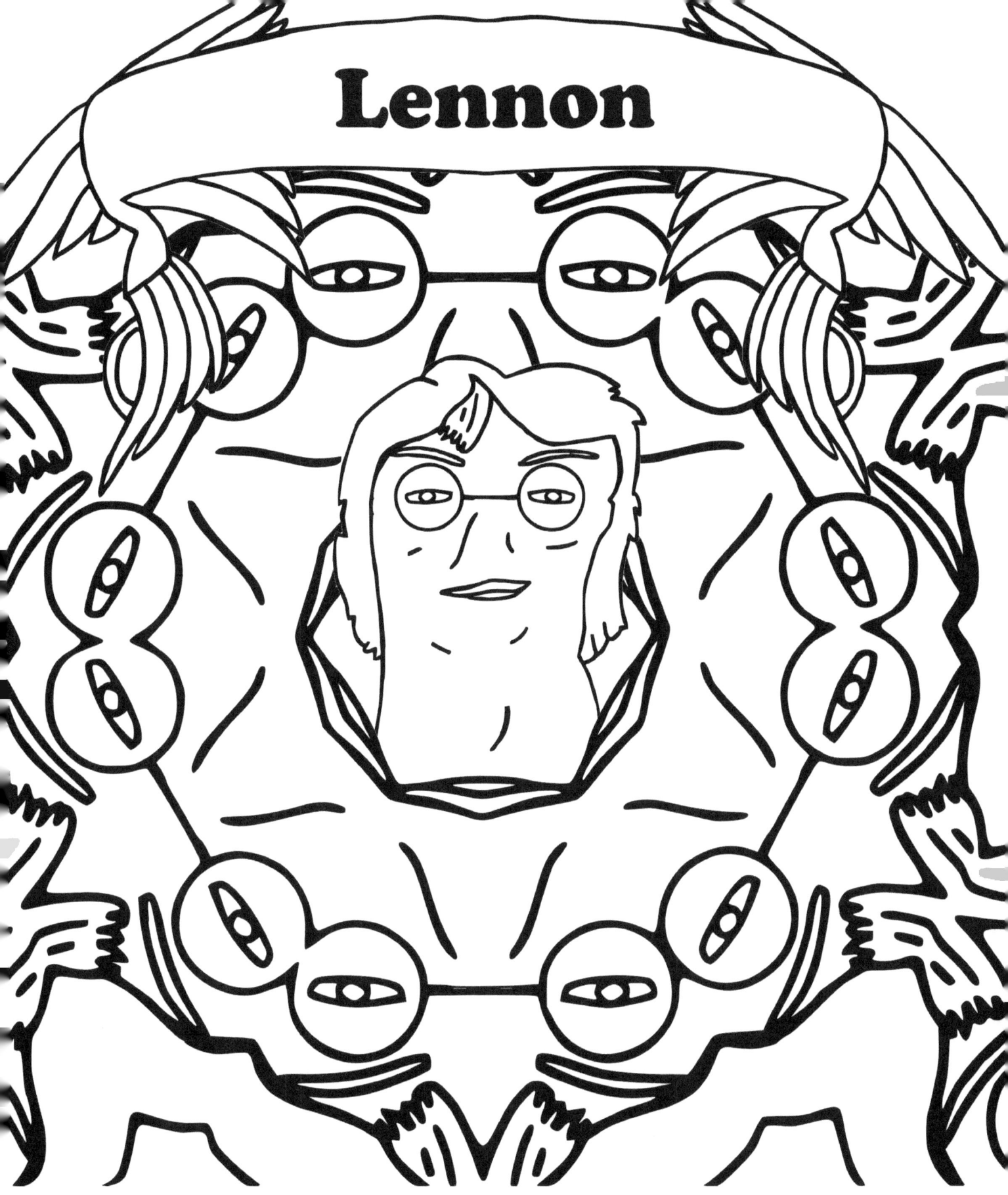

"Reality leaves a lot to the imagination."

Koba

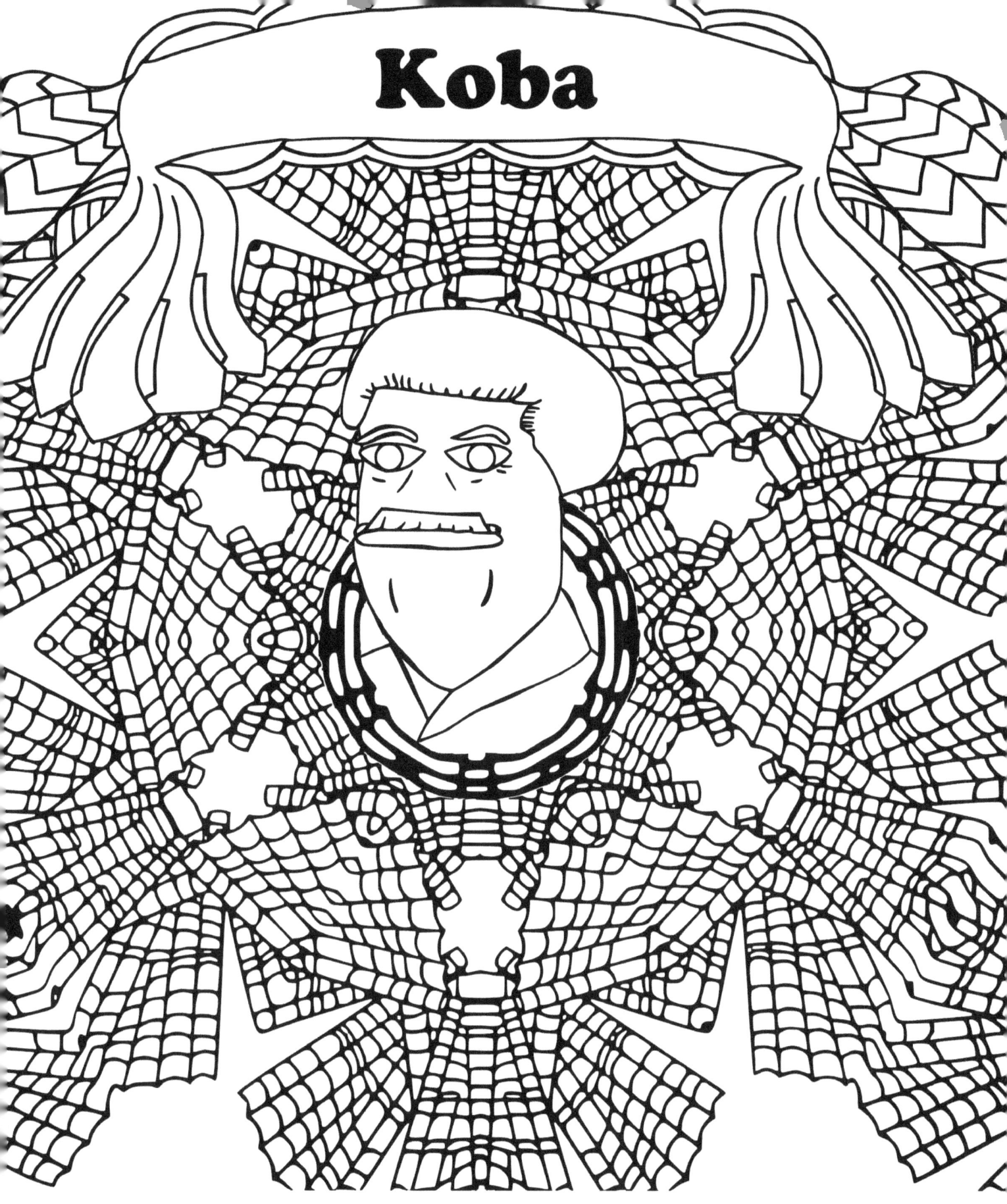

"The writer is the engineer of the human soul."

Dear Father

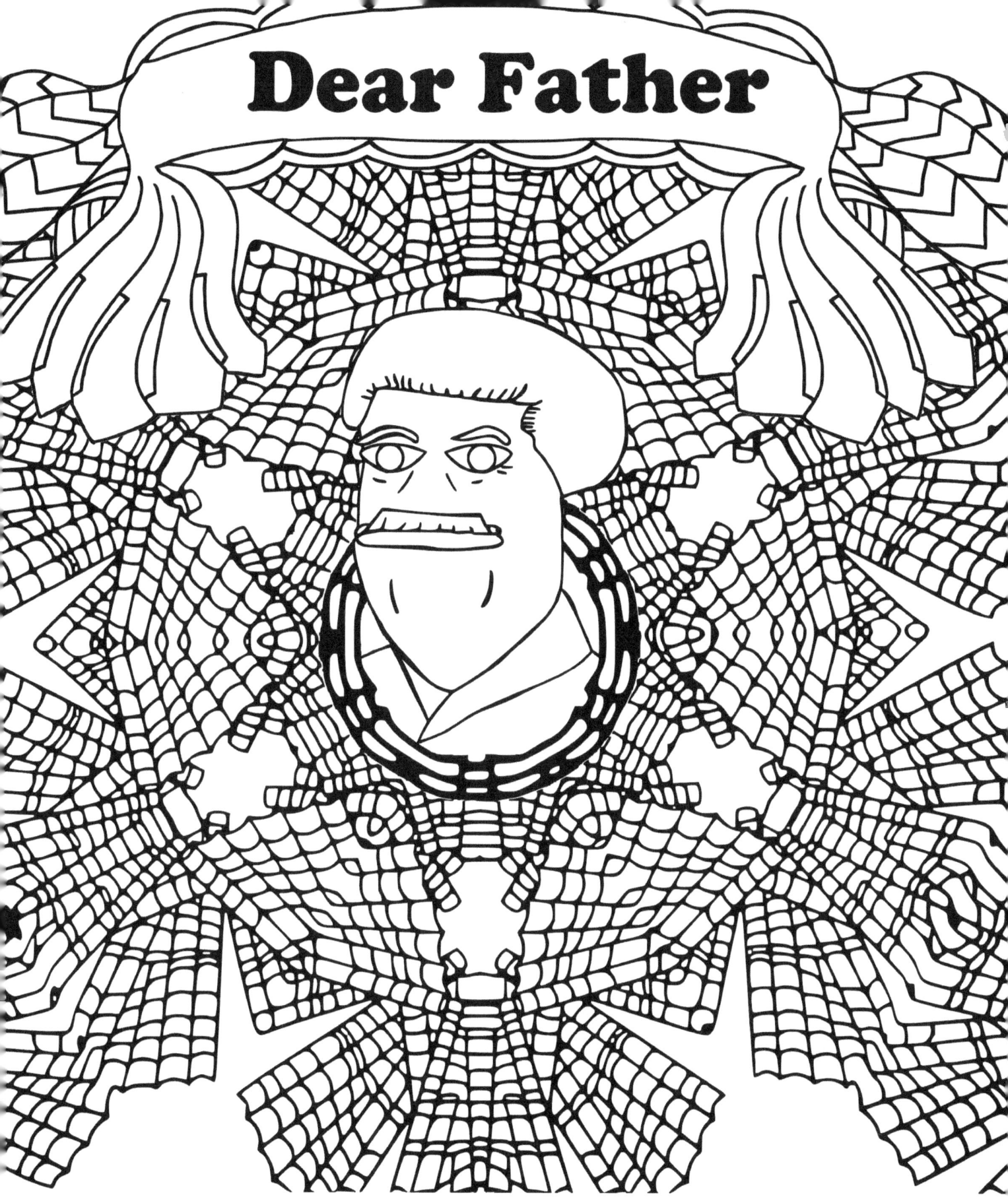

"We don't let them have ideas. Why would we let them have guns?"

Wacko Bird

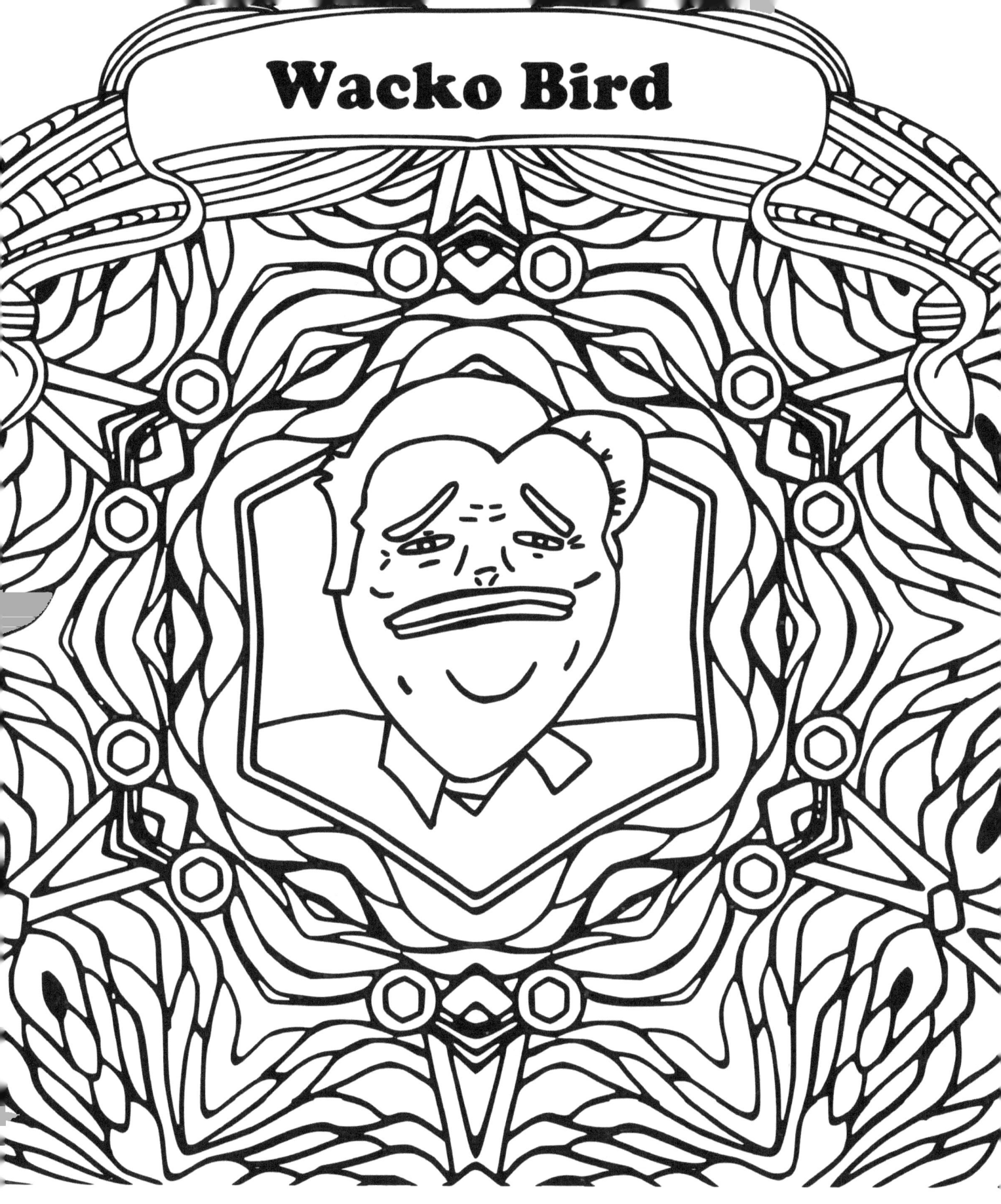

"I was bitten by an octopus."

Creepy Dracula

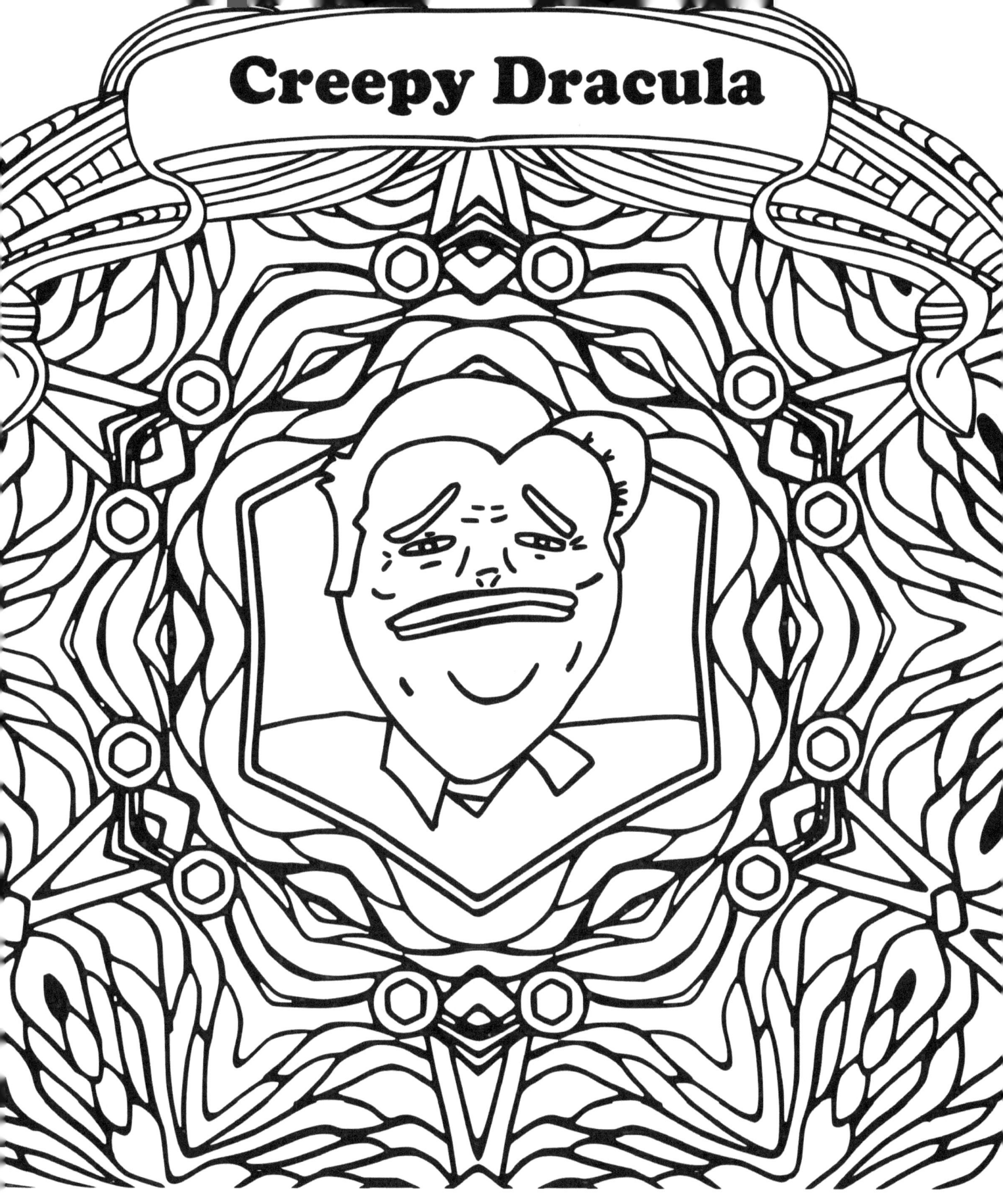

"Back to Happy Valley."

Dynamite

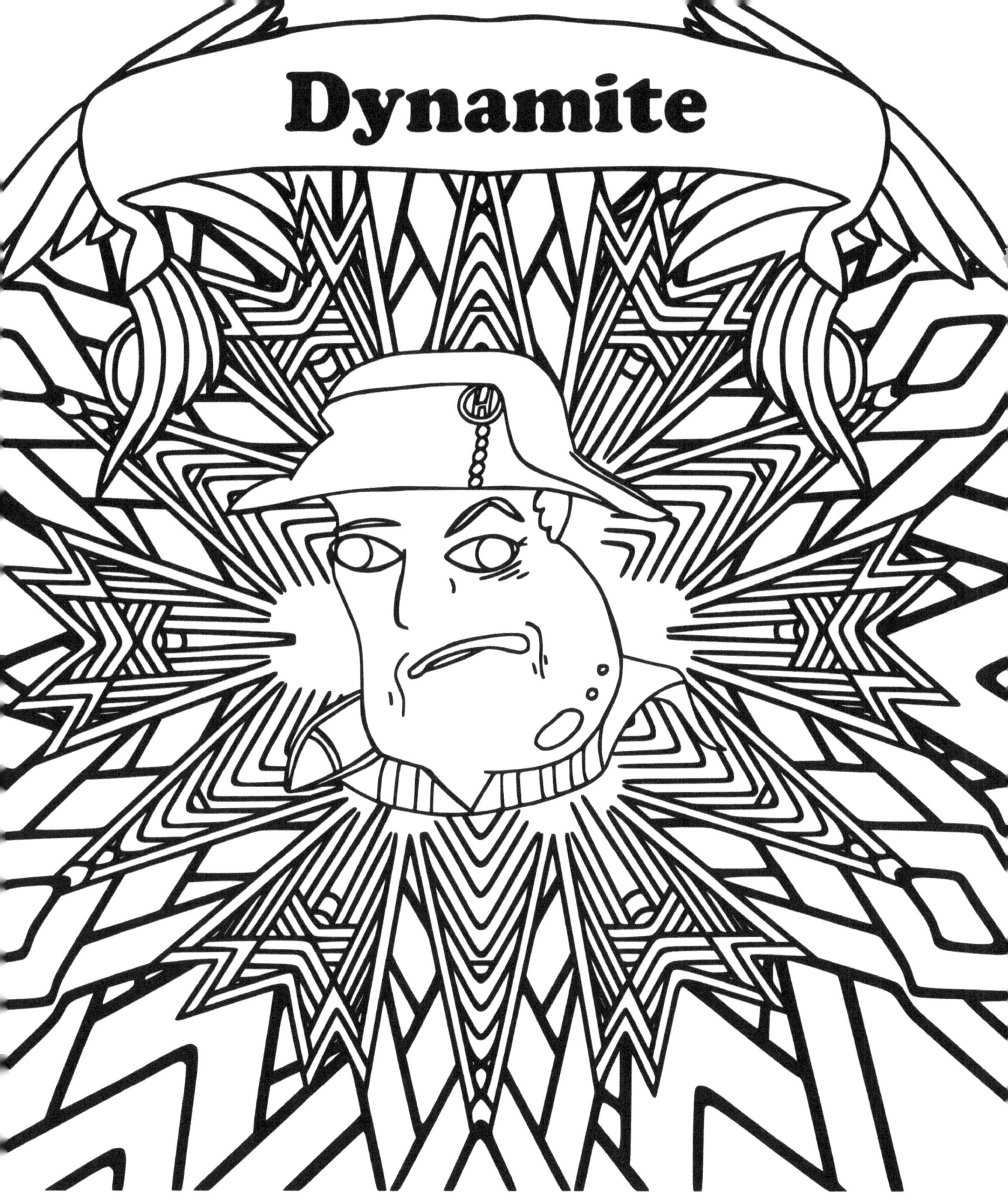

"The best way to keep one's word is not to give it."

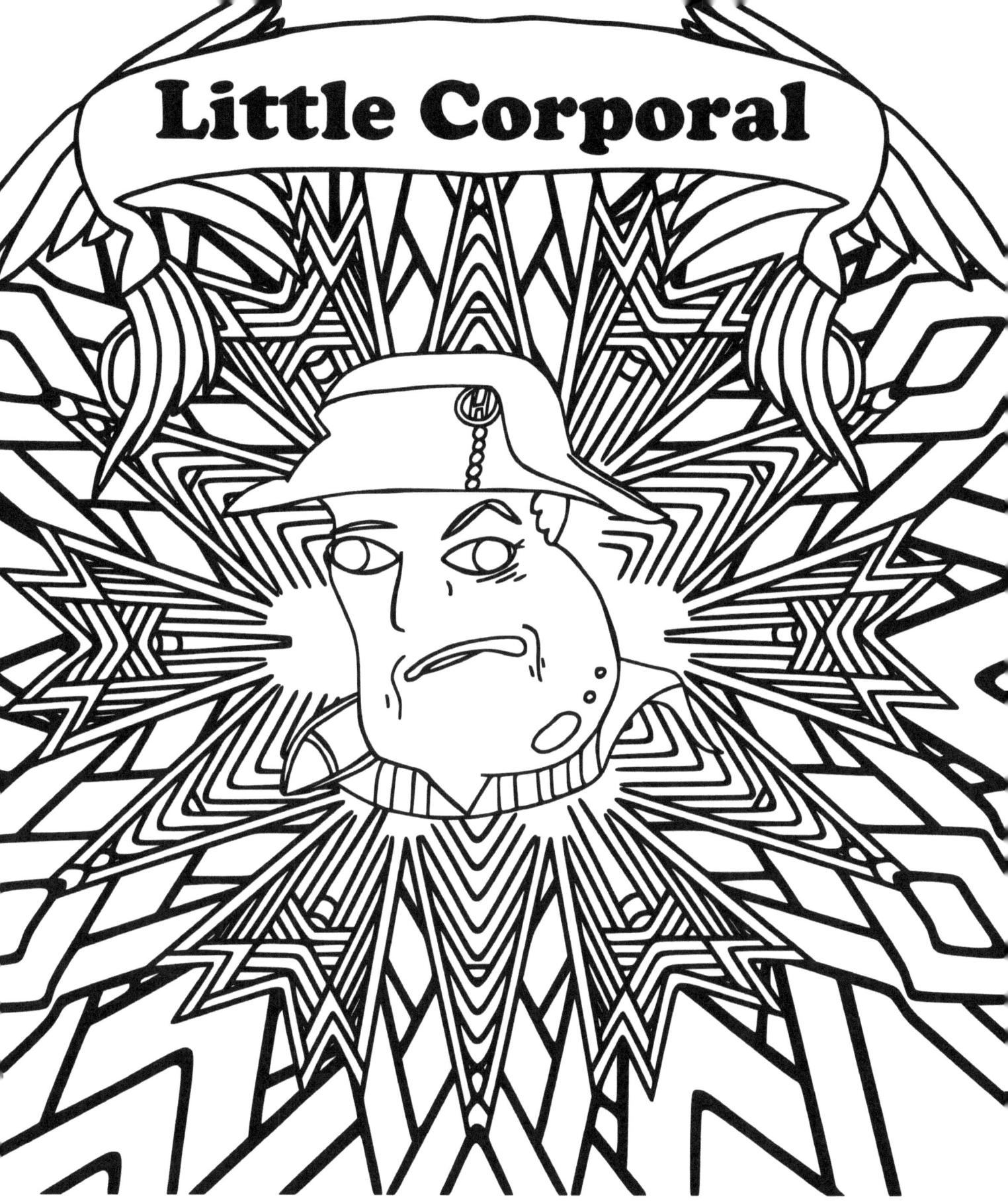

Little Corporal

"In politics stupidity is not a handicap."

Philos

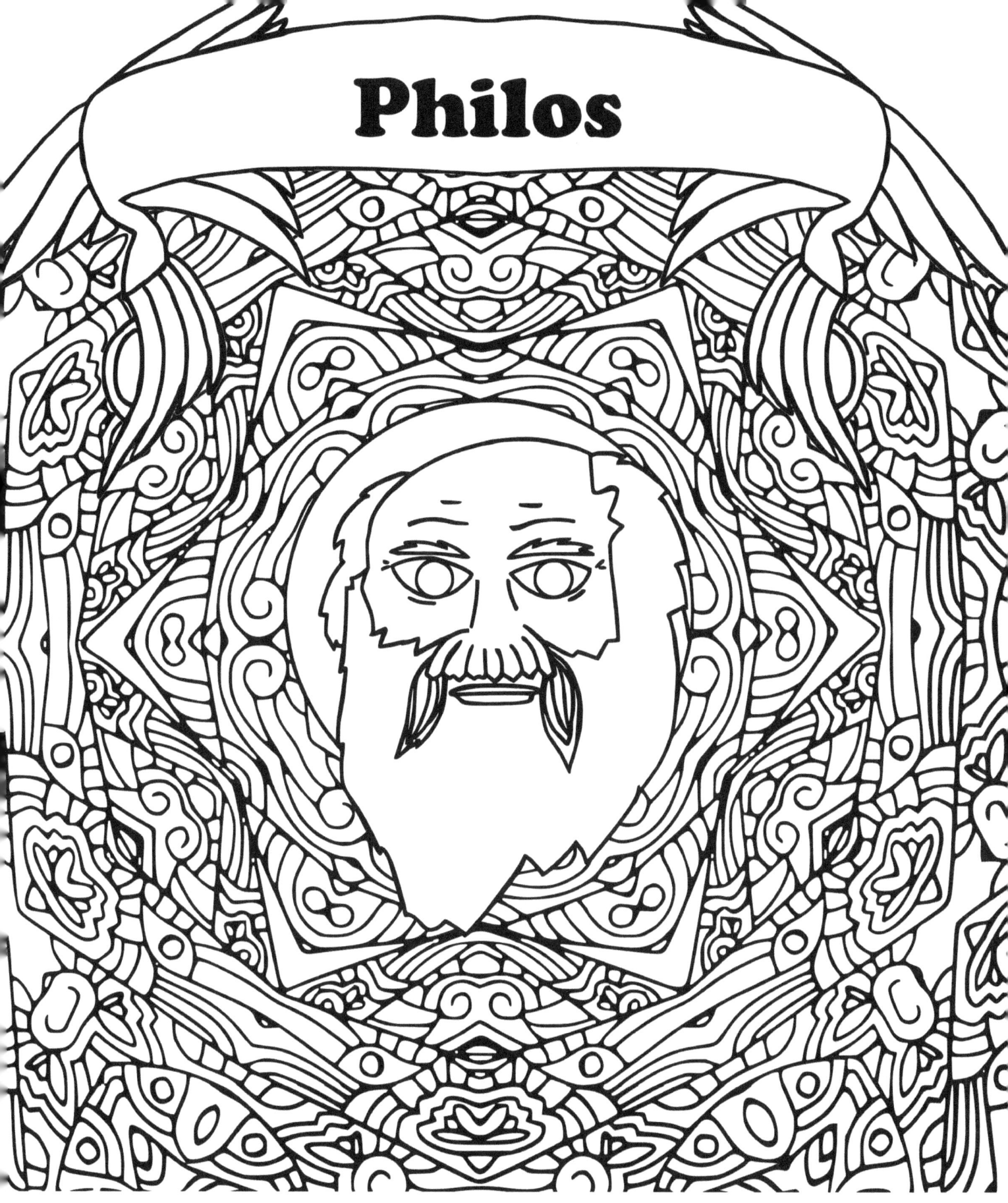

"A scientific man ought to have no wishes, no affections, - a mere heart of stone."

Gas

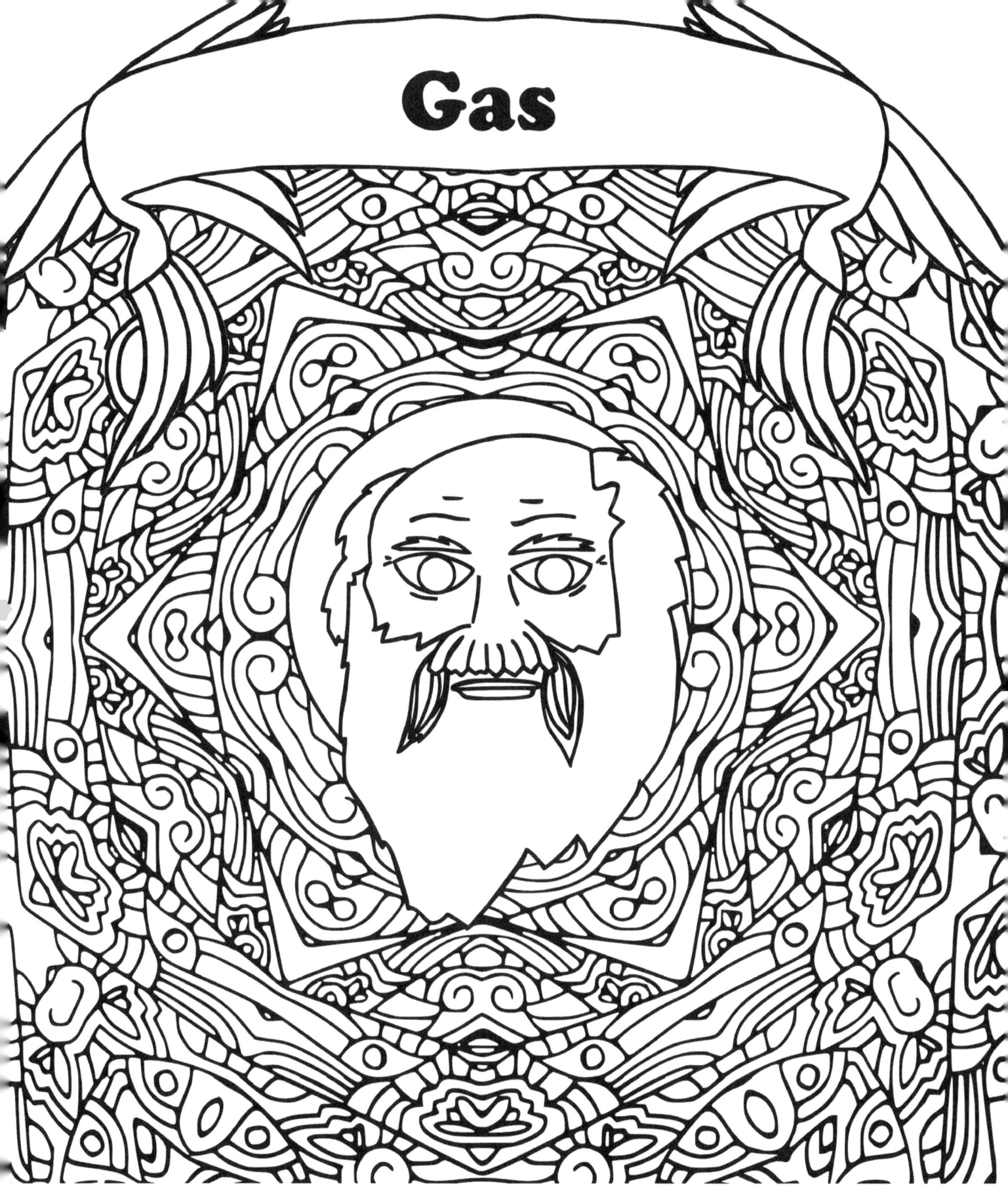

"I love fools' experiments. I am always making them."

Vlad the Impaler

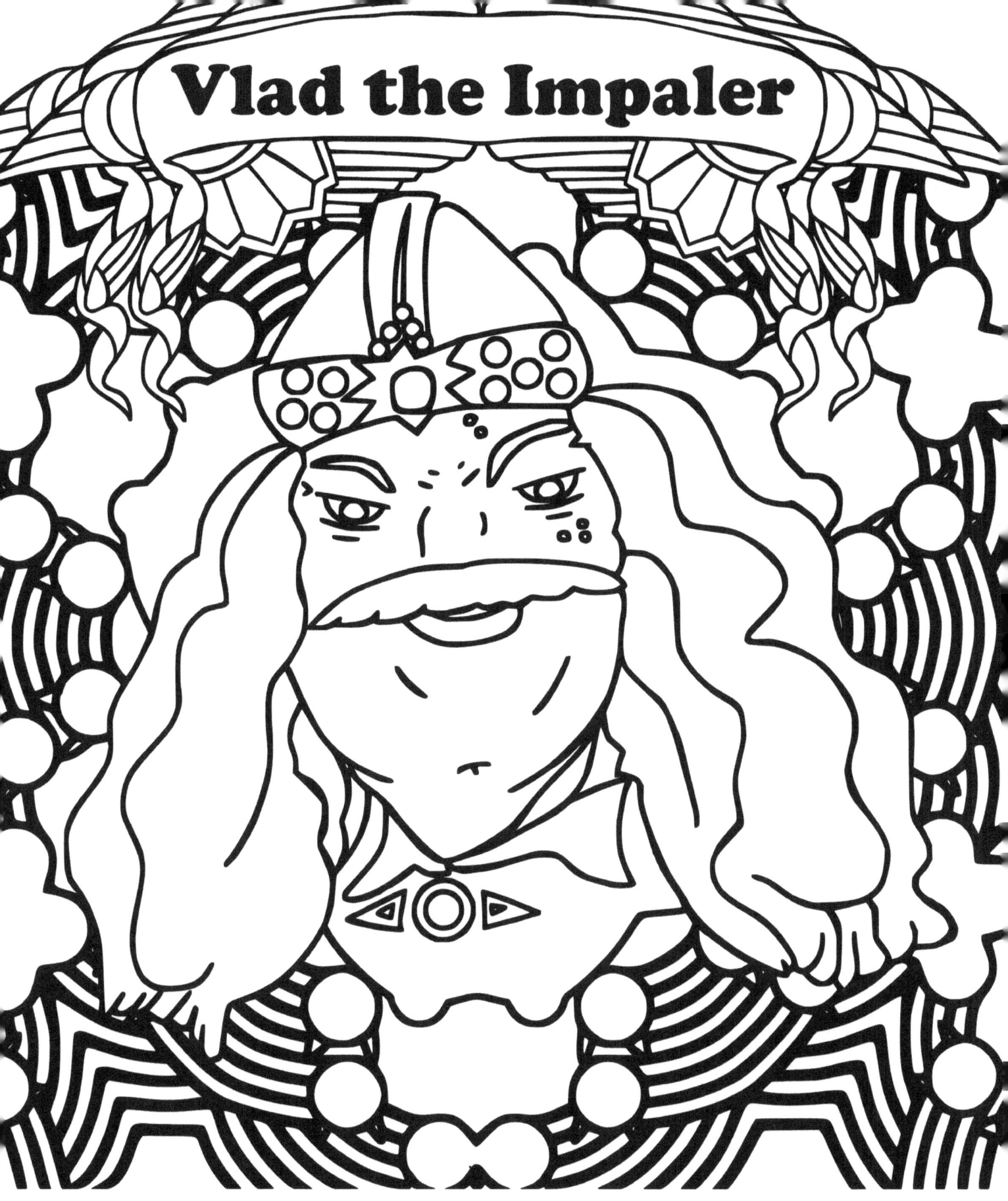

"You know where you can stick it!"

Vlad Tepes

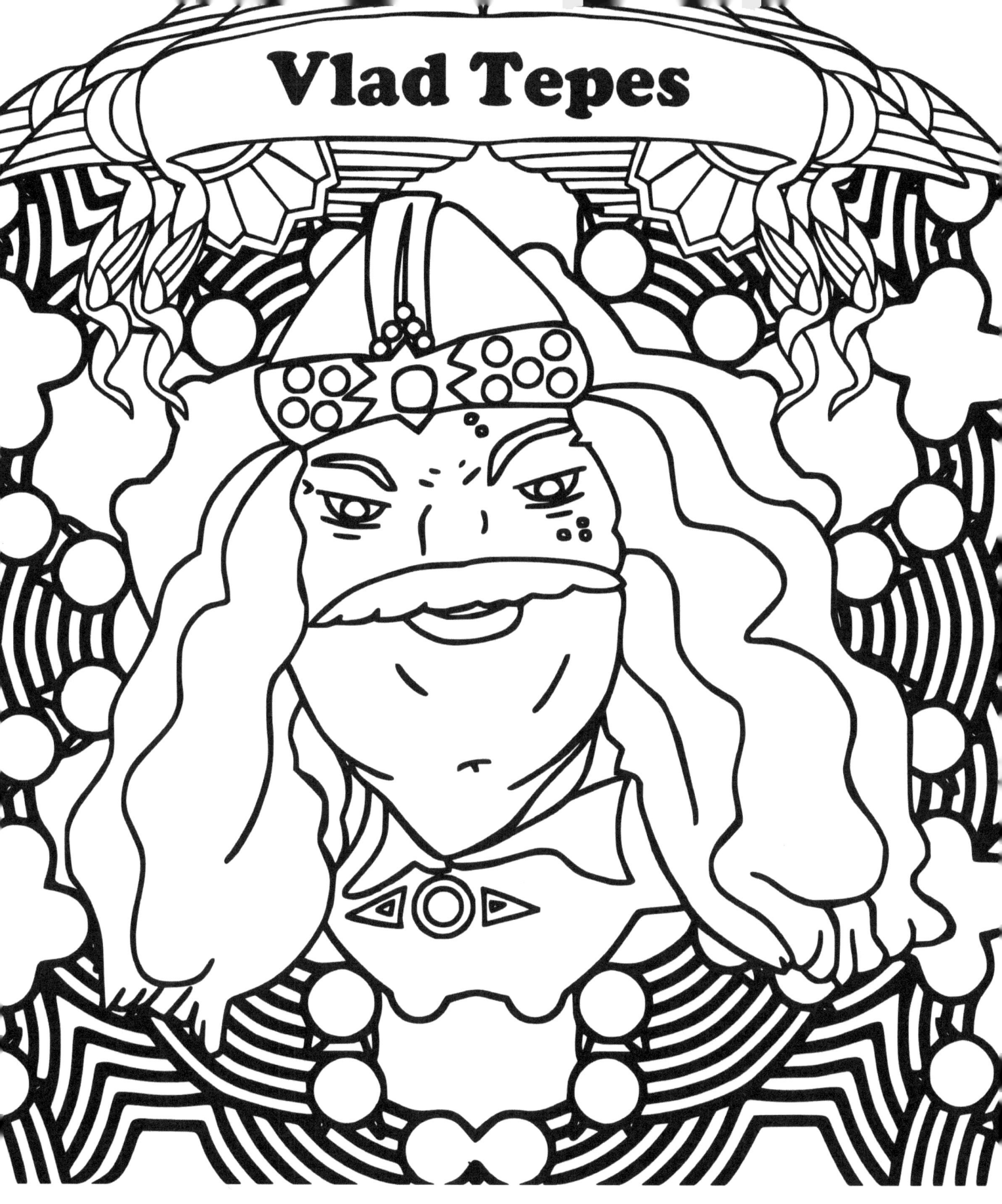

"You got blood on you."

Bapu

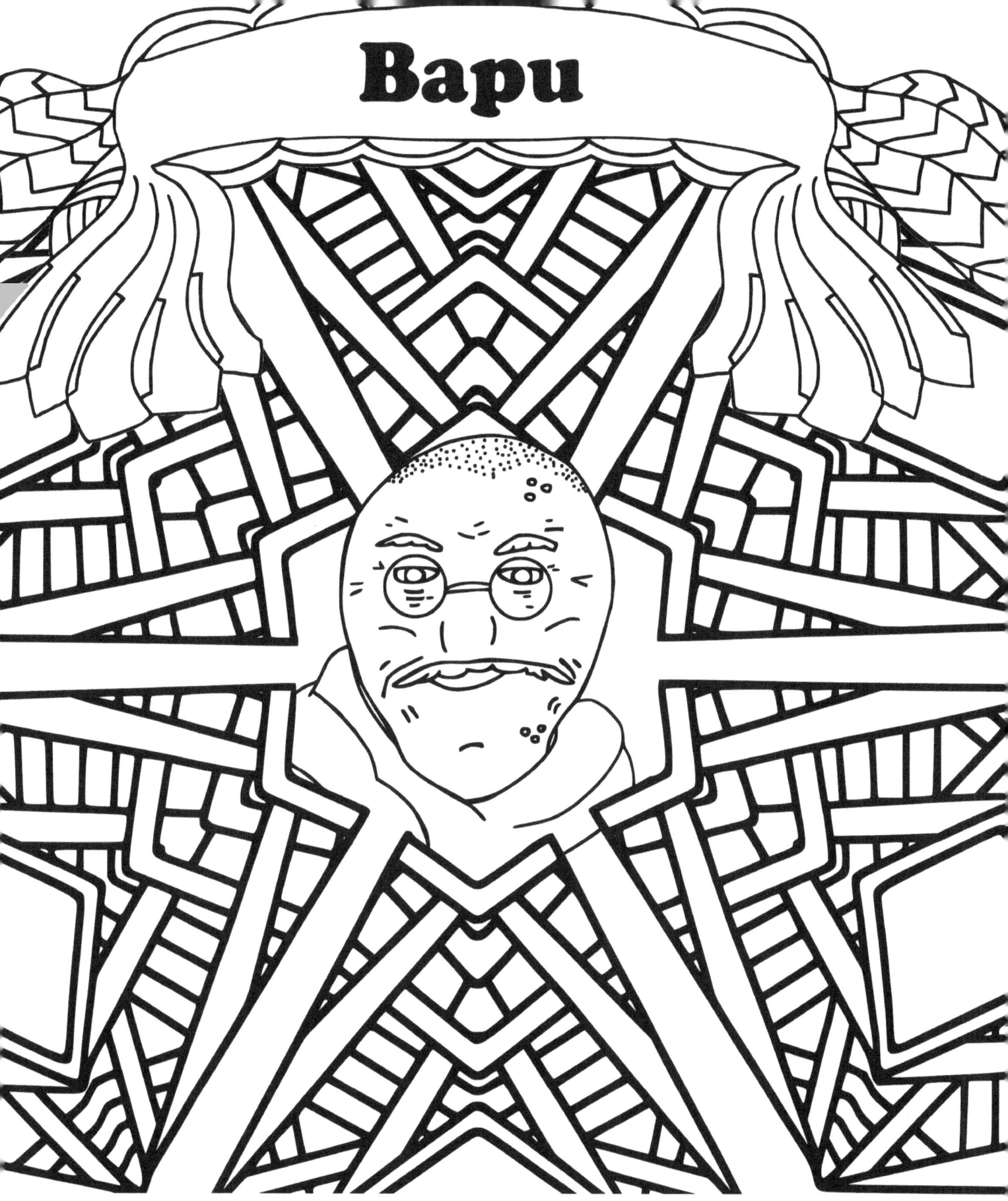

"First they ignore you, then they laugh at you, then they fight you, then you win."

Mahatma

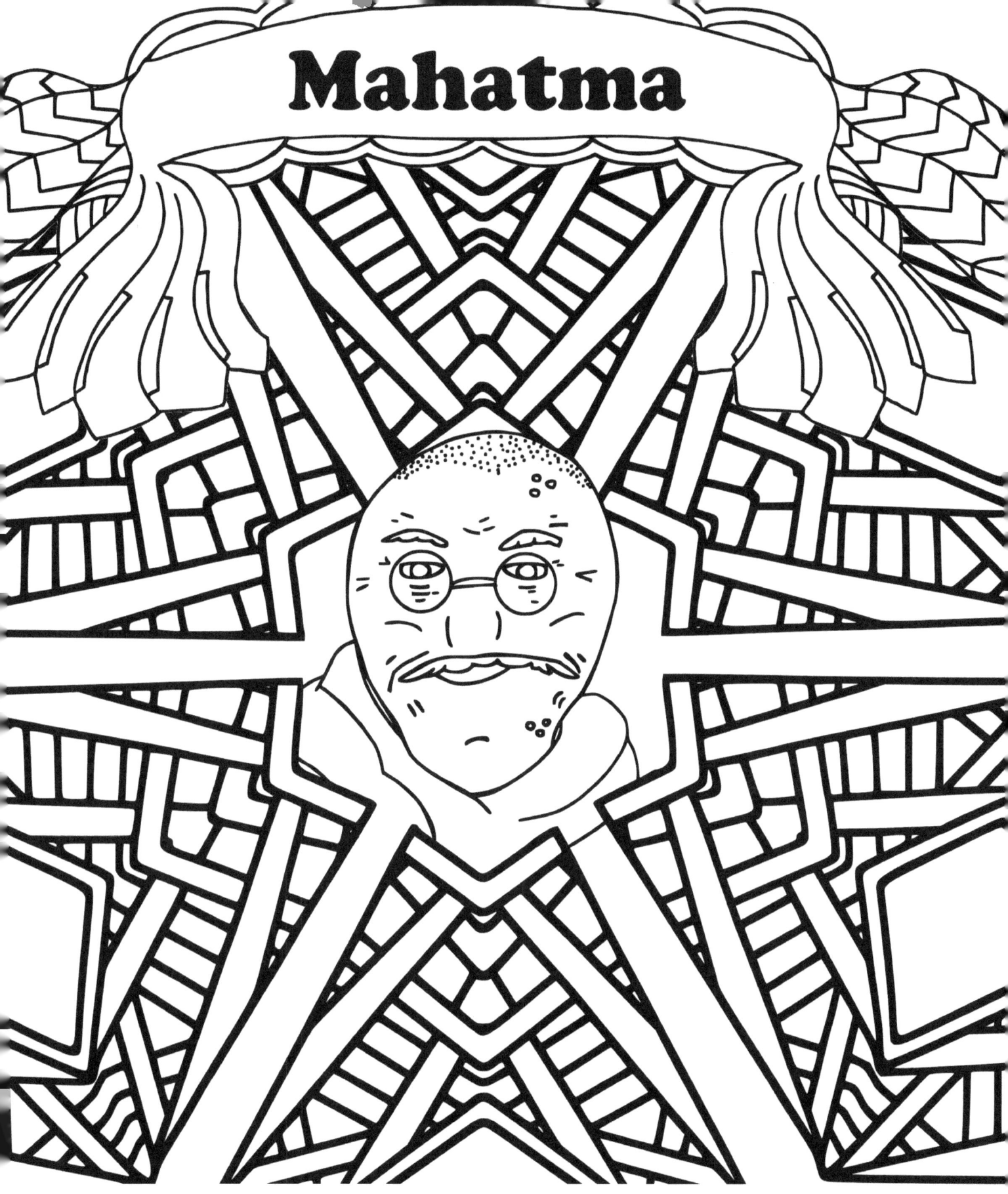

"My life is my message."

Boz

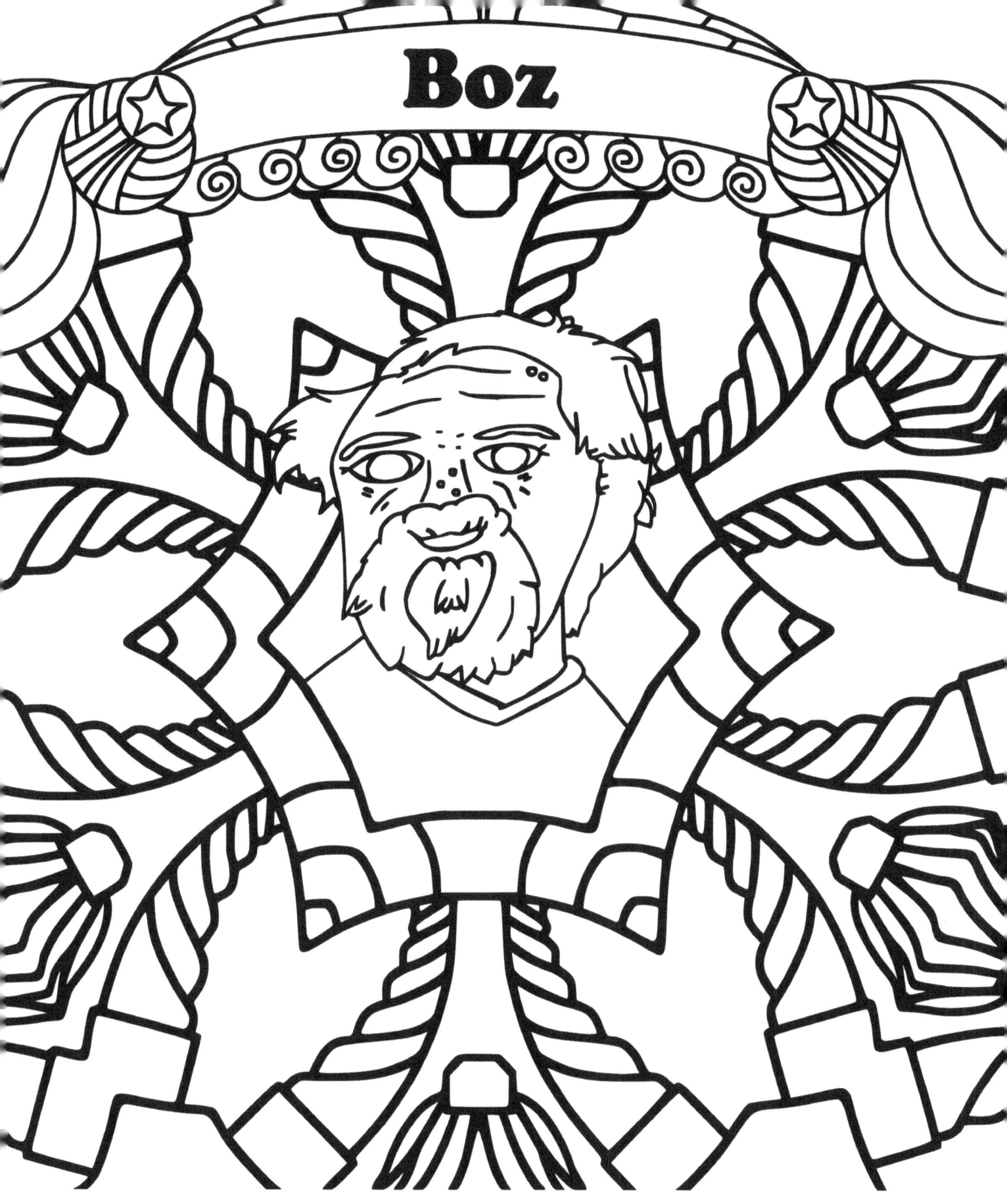

"He would make a lovely corpse."

Dickens

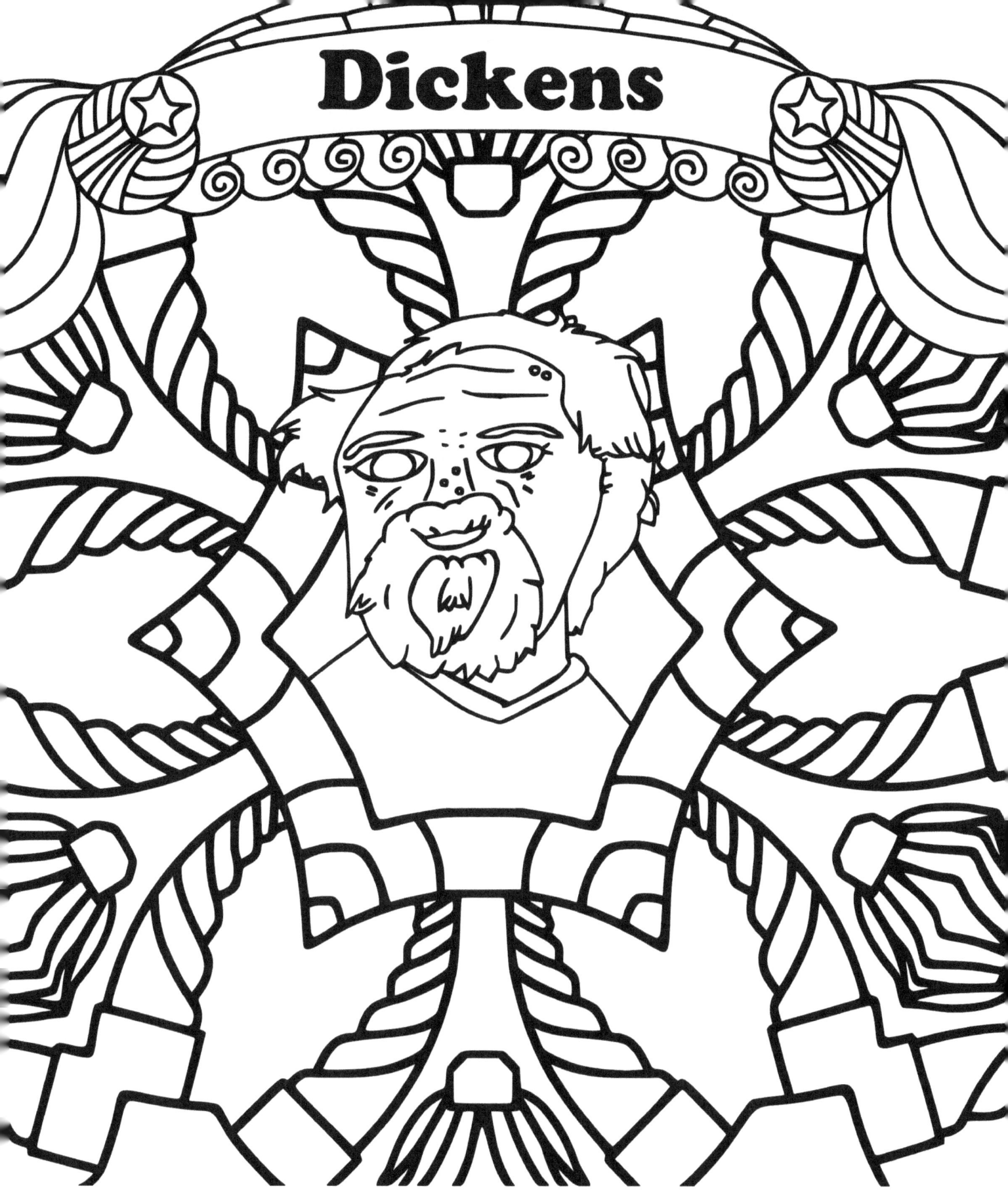

"A loving heart is truest wisdom."

Angie

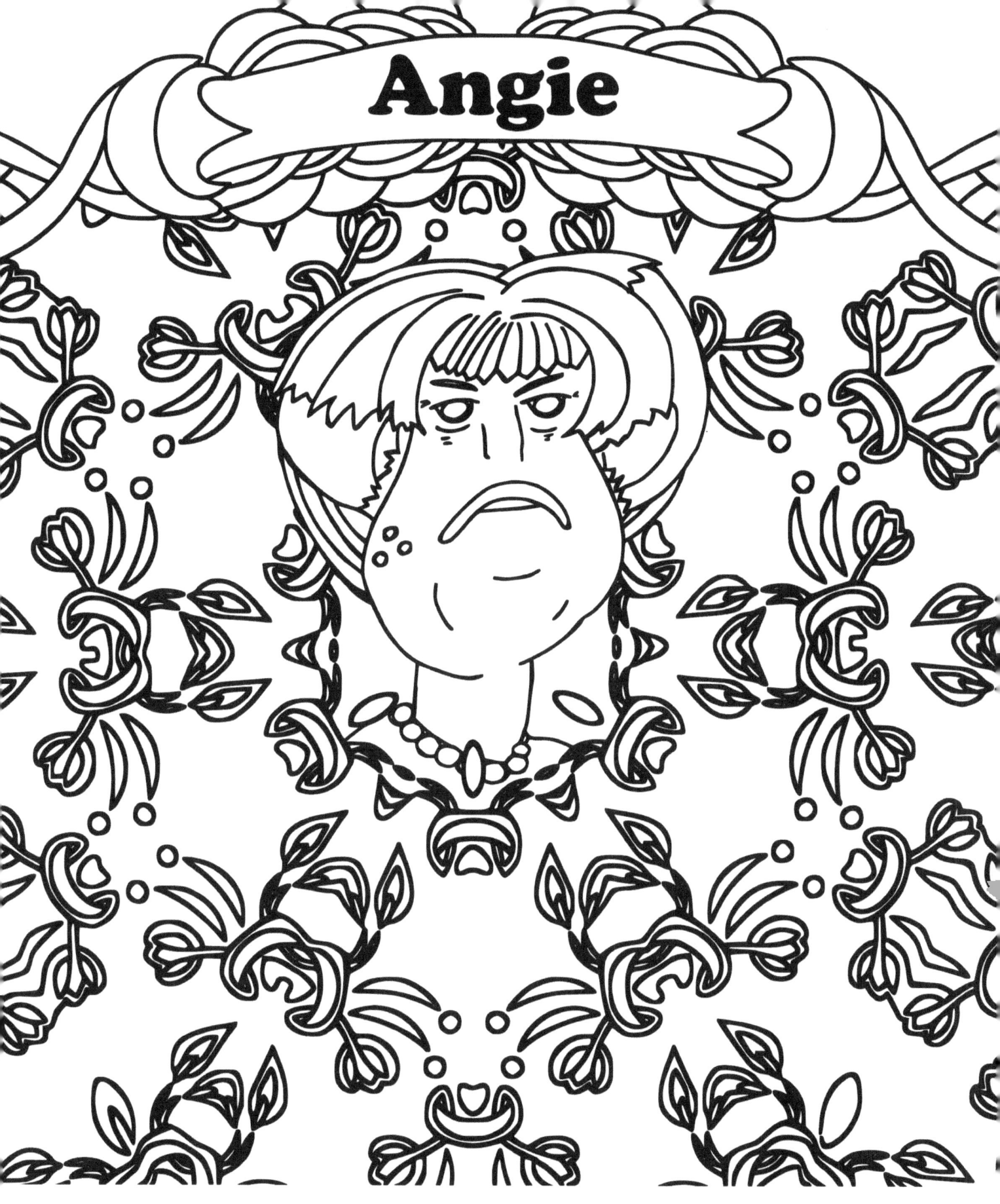

"Spying among friends is never acceptable."

Mutti

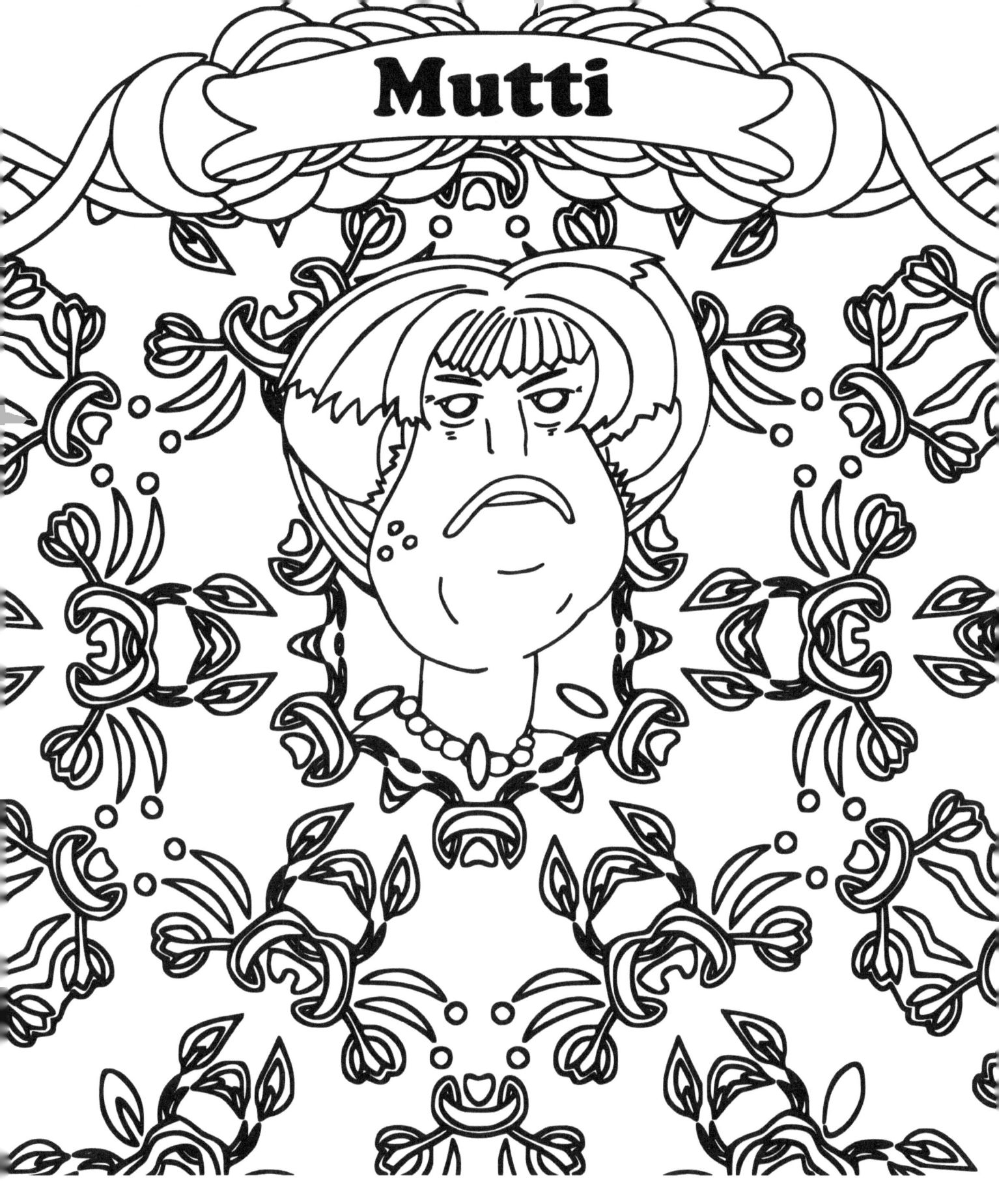

"We will cope."

Fabulous

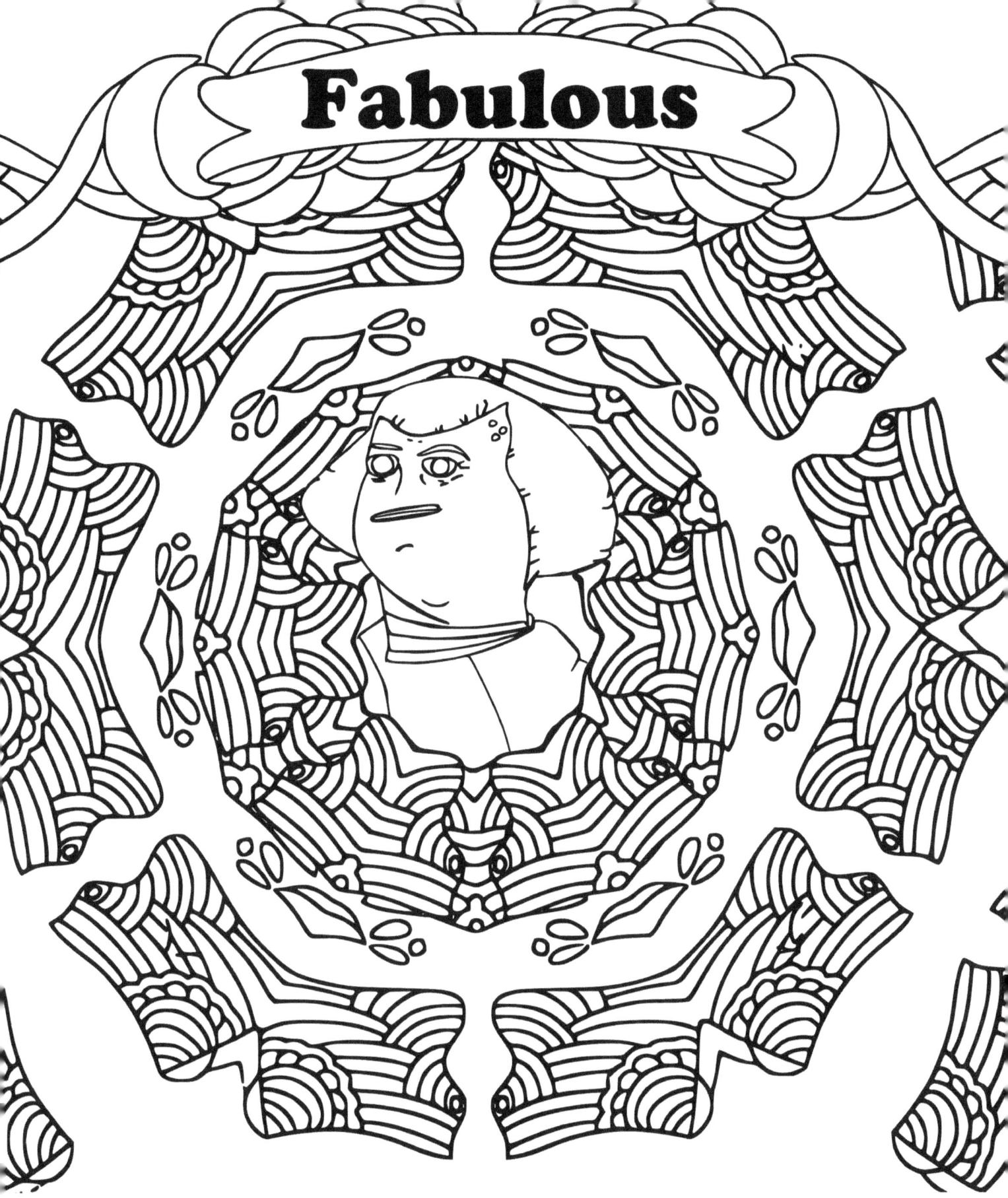

"It is better to offer no excuse than a bad one."

Washington

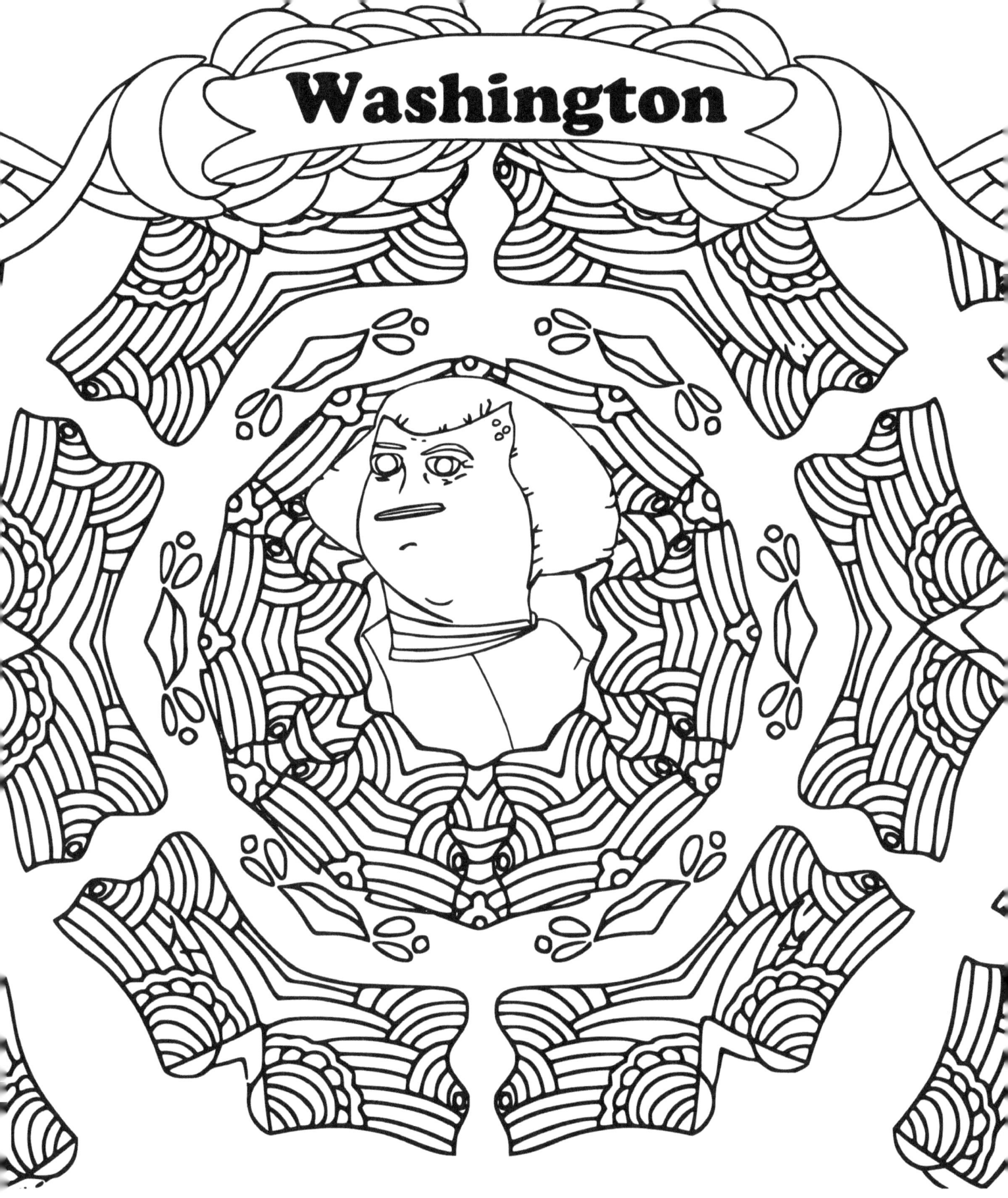

"It is far better to be alone, than to be in bad company."

The Old Man

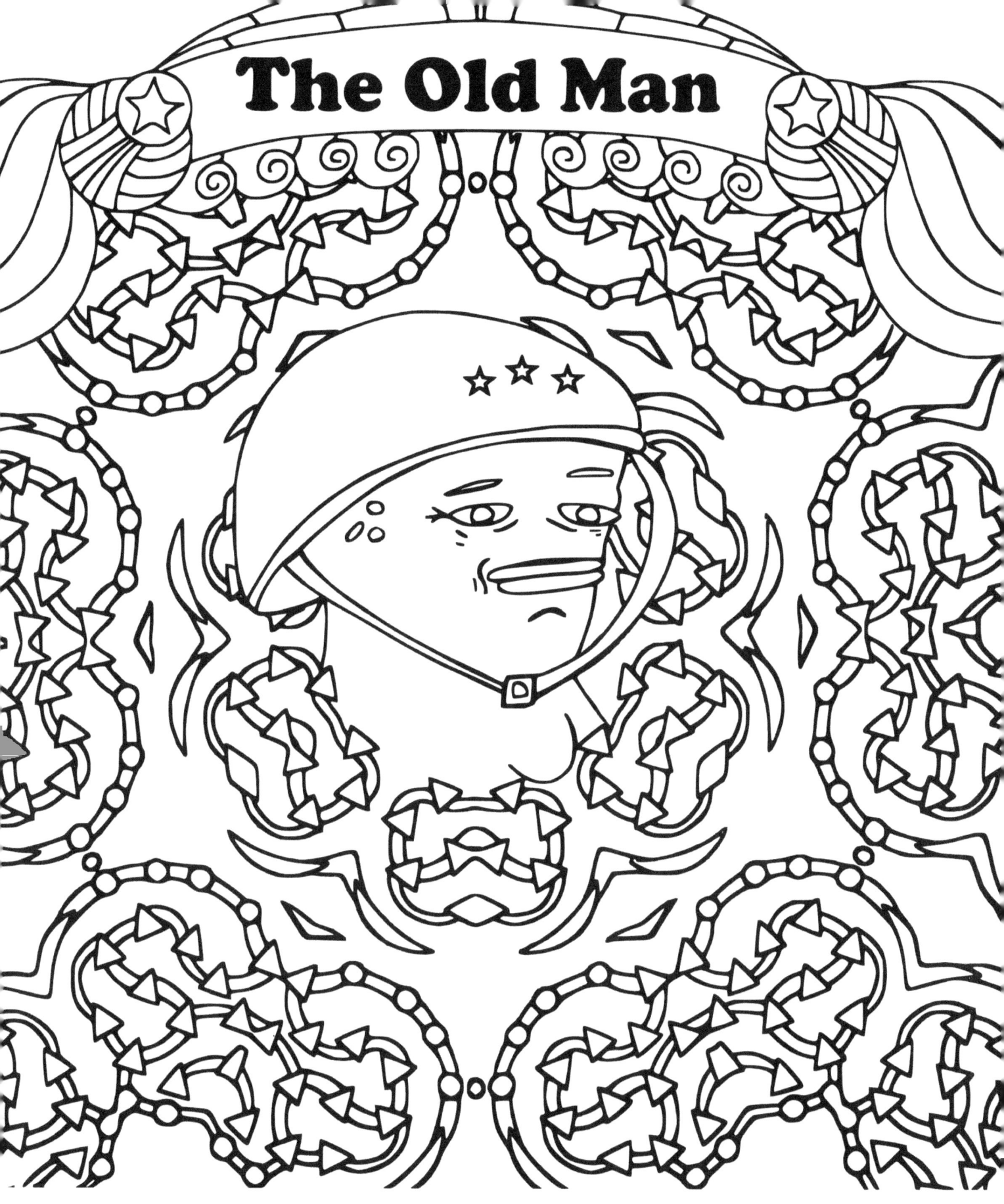

"A pint of sweat will save a gallon of blood."

Old Gibs

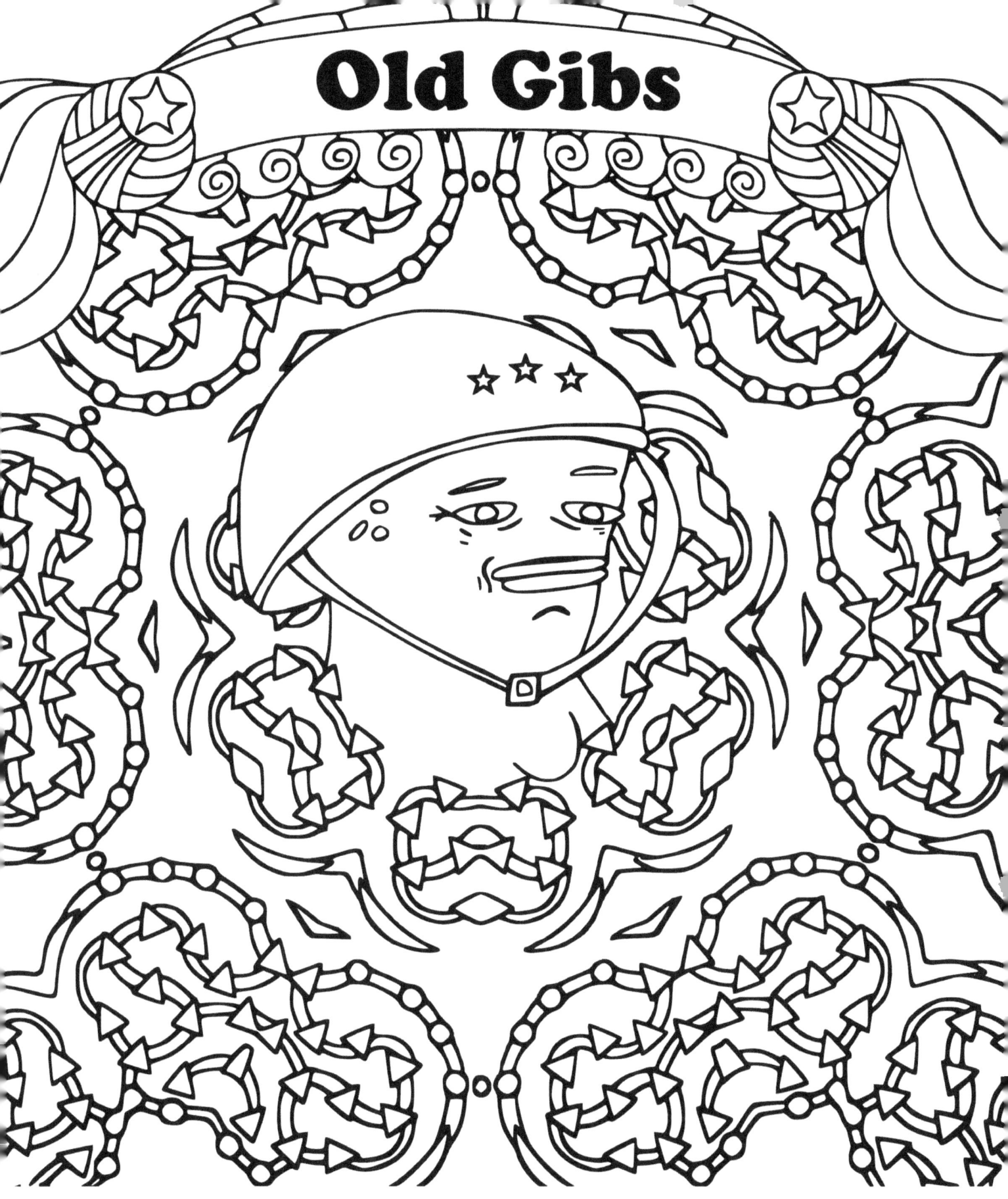

"Better to fight for something than live for nothing."

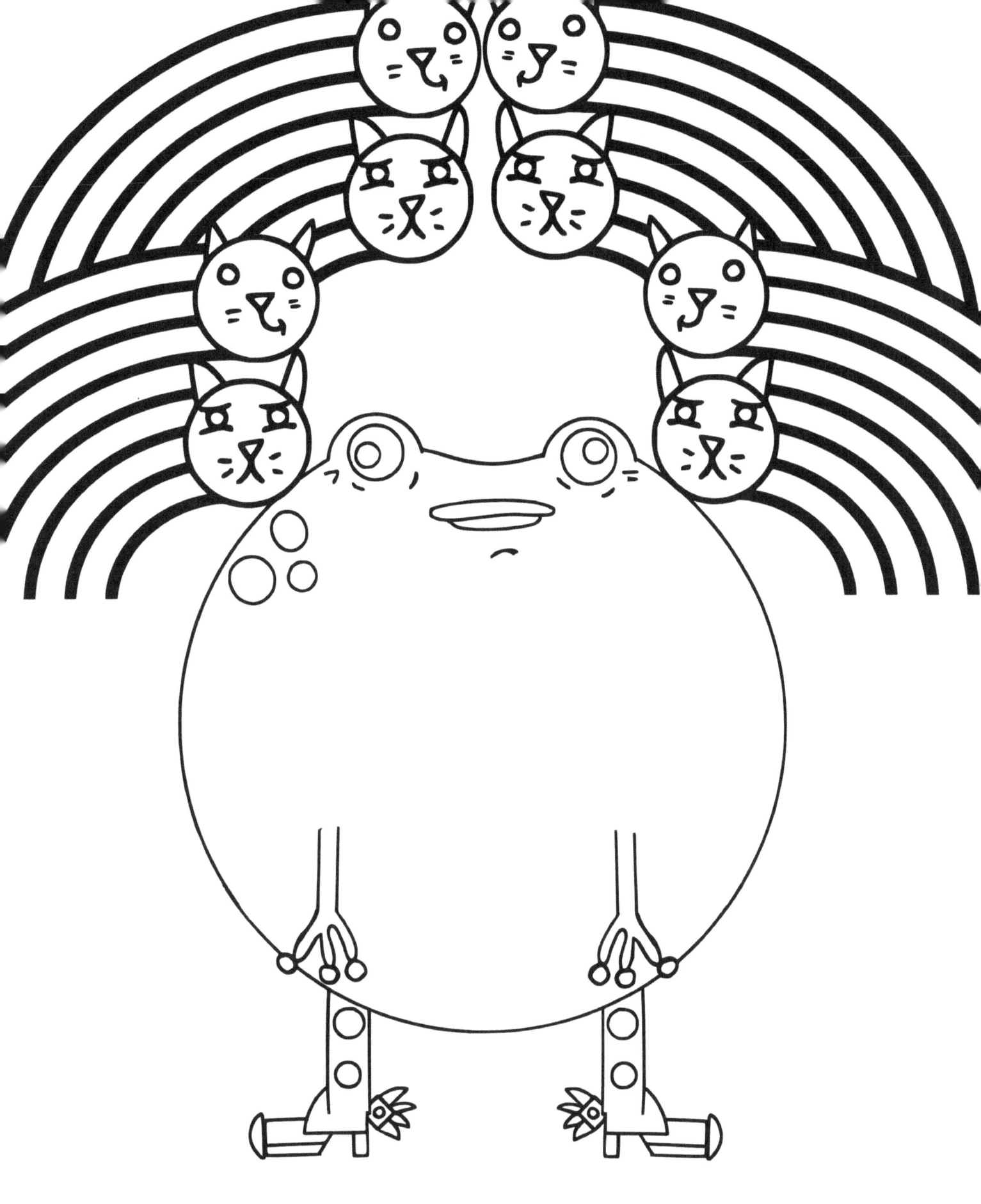

You're Awesome!

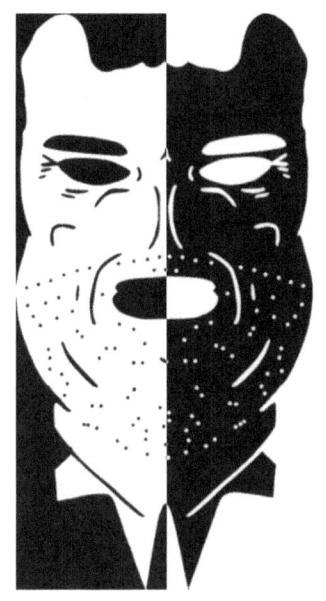

J.D. LUKE